"*Sing Your Own Song* is a refreshing celebration of family and community. Cynthia Orange proposes practical ways single moms can take care of themselves as they journey from new moms to empty nesters."

David Wilmes, author of *Parenting for Prevention*

"With tender prose and a thoughtful eye, Cynthia Orange examines the lives of our greatest warriors: single moms. *Sing Your Own Song* is a soulful, unvarnished, and uplifting guide. Through stories, anecdotes, and well-anchored encouragement, it cleanses away the stigmas and self-doubts of single motherhood. This is a must-read for any mother, single or otherwise. Make that any father too."

—Peter Kotz, editor of *Cleveland Scene*

"Single mothers not only need each other, they need informed friends and family who understand this complex and sometimes overwhelming journey. Cynthia Orange's wise and witty book helps me be such a friend. I learned a lot reading it."

—Christina Baldwin, author of *Life's Companion,
Journal Writing As a Spiritual Quest*, and *Calling
the Circle: The First and Future Culture*

"I found myself wanting to sit at the kitchen table with Cynthia Orange and share my own stories. She's absolutely trustworthy, honest, humble, and wise. Thank you for creating a book that reads like a talk with my grandmother *and* feels like a trip to the resource center for single moms."

—Ann Linnea, single mom and author of *Deep Water Passage— A Spiritual Journey at Midlife* and *Teaching Kids to Love the Earth*

"Cynthia Orange offers a song for single mothers, with lyrics that touch the fine range between the practical and the poetic. With generosity of spirit and no malice toward men, this book brings fresh breath and range to a subject that, in the past, has been overpoliticized and underappreciated. Single moms, and the men who know them, will find solace and illumination in these pages."

—Richard Louv, author of *The Web of Life: Weaving the Values That Sustain Us*

Sing Your Own Song

A Guide for Single Moms

Cynthia Orange

HAZELDEN®

INFORMATION & EDUCATIONAL SERVICES

Hazelden
Center City, Minnesota 55012-0176

1-800-328-0094
1-651-213-4590 (Fax)
www.hazelden.org

Library of Congress Cataloging-in-Publication Data
Orange, Cynthia.
    Sing your own song : a guide for single moms / Cynthia Orange.
      p. cm.
    Includes bibliographic references and index.
    ISBN 1-56838-572-2 (pbk.)
    1. Single mothers—United States—Psychology. 2. Single mothers—
      United States—Life skills guides. 3. Single-parent families—United
      States. 4. Self-help techniques—United States. I. Title.

HQ759.915 .O73 2001
646.7′0085′2—dc21
                                        00-065896

05   04   03   02   01   6   5   4   3   2   1

Cover design by David Spohn
Interior design by Elizabeth Cleveland
Typesetting by Stanton Publication Services, Inc.

AUTHOR'S NOTE

The stories excerpted throughout this book are based on actual experiences, relayed to me through interviews and conversations or in response to questionnaires distributed to current and former single mothers, adult children who lived for some period of time in single mother households, and professionals who work with single-parent families. They are presented anonymously to protect the privacy of the people involved. In some cases, minor details have been changed to ensure anonymity.

THIS BOOK IS DEDICATED TO

my daughter, Jessica,
my mother, Florence,
and to the memory of my Grandma Reeck

strong women all, who taught me
what it means to be a mother

Contents

Acknowledgments

I wish to thank all my friends who opened their hearts to tell their stories to me and who helped me gather the stories of others. I thank all the current and former single moms and the adult children of single mothers who took the time to share their experiences and memories. I know that for some of you revisiting those early days was a mixture of joy and pain. Know that your words and wisdom make a difference.

Special thanks go to Vince and Scott, for their sound advice and good counsel. To Lisa, for those "launching lunches" that got things on their way. To Patty, whose stories and laughter continue to make my life richer. To Ruth and Chris, my gentle taskmasters who kept me on track. To Dianna, for her professional input and personal support. To Cori, who was always so generous with her time, guidance, and friendship. To my sister Dianne for her contributions and constant encouragement. And thanks to Liv and Beth, my writing companions and good friends, who never fail to make my work better.

I want to also thank Bette Nowacki and Tracy Snyder, my patient and good-natured editors, and all my other friends at Hazelden who have enriched my life for fifteen years now and from whom I continue to learn and grow.

And, finally, I am eternally grateful for the unwavering support, love, and assistance my husband, Michael, gives me in everything I undertake. He is my most loyal fan, my most honest critic, and my most trusted friend.

Introduction

◨ ◨ ◨

It is raining as I write this. It is early March in Minnesota and the weather this winter has been wildly unpredictable: seventy-two degrees with seamless sunny sky yesterday; powerful thunderstorms today with dropping temperatures; possible snow tonight. It is difficult to know from one day to the next how to dress to go outside; whether to slip on a light cotton dress, a soft fleece outfit, or jeans and a down vest.

This morning I awoke to the crack of thunder and the pounding of rain and rose to see the bird feeders in the front yard swinging on the leafless branches. It looked cold and dreary. I listened to the weather forecast and looked at the weather map in the newspaper, gathering the information I needed to better plan my day. Yet, no matter how well I prepare myself, there is no guarantee that I will not get a little chilled or a bit damp today.

Life as a single mother is like a Minnesota March. There might be glorious days of sunshine and warmth, turbulent and troublesome stretches of unpredictable weather, and cold and lonely times when it is tempting to crawl back into bed and pull a heavy comforter over your head to keep the world at bay. But there are things you can do, precautions you can take, and information you can gather to help prepare for the uncertainties and challenges of single motherhood.

That's what this book is all about. It's an afghan, a thermometer, and an umbrella. It's meant to comfort, inform, and protect single mothers and their children. There is an old Irish tradition of the *anamchara*, or soul friend—a spiritual guide

1

who helps individuals on their life journeys. Ideally, this book will be embraced by readers as a wise and nonjudgmental "soul friend" who educates and inspires, affirms and supports, and offers mothers practical and creative ways to take good care of themselves and their children.

Single-parent families are no oddity in this society. According to the U.S. Bureau of the Census in 1998, 19.8 million children under the age of eighteen (almost 28 percent of American children) lived with one parent, and the majority of these children (84 percent) lived with their mothers. Whether you are a single mother by choice, by chance, or by circumstances such as divorce or widowhood, know that you are in the company of millions of other single moms.

We need to rethink the outdated, 1950s idea that "family" means a father who works full-time, a mother who may or may not work outside the home, and their children. There's certainly nothing wrong with that picture of family, but it's just one snapshot among many in today's American family album that now holds very different family portraits. Today, women alone and women together raise children, just as men alone and men together raise children. Grandparents raise children. And men and women, married and unmarried, raise children. They are all families, and they all deserve respect and praise. This book celebrates and addresses the concerns of one family possibility among many: the single mother family.

We need to create a more inclusive definition of family that better reflects what so many of you and your children are actually living. There is no longer a one-family-fits-all formula or ideal, if there ever was. When myths are exposed as myths, they lose their power because we realize we cannot compete with or ever hope to attain what is an illusion. When we let go of the unrealistic expectations that surround the myths of what a family *should be,* we are free to celebrate the families we actually have. When we affirm to ourselves and others that single mothers and their children are genuine families just as they are at this moment in time—not *broken families* or *families in transition,* as some would have us believe—we can approach the world with confidence instead of apology.

The times are indeed changing. More and more single mothers are being praised instead of scorned. In fact, one of them—Dorothy Day, the left-wing Catholic heroine and unwed mother who dedicated her life to helping the poor and homeless—is being considered for sainthood. Contemporary women such as celebrity talk-show host Rosie O'Donnell, who has adopted three children as a single mom, are viewed today as positive role models. One child of a single mother—Bill Clinton, whose father was killed in a traffic accident before he was born—grew up to be president of the United States.

While I know the chances are slim that single mothers who read this book will be considered for sainthood, or become television stars, or see your sons or daughters become president, you and your children can achieve your own version of stardom. This book is filled with success stories of single mothers and their children—*families*—who grew strong and flourished in their single-parent homes. Their examples and the ideas from a variety of other expert sources create a compass for single mothers who are steering a similar course.

I hope the book will also be a prevention tool. Single mothers, like anyone else who juggles the often overwhelming responsibilities and challenges of life, are vulnerable to stress-related illnesses, to depression, and to addiction or other unhealthy behavior. If just one reader uses a suggestion contained in this book at a time of stress or confusion instead of pouring a drink, popping a pill, or engaging in some other potentially harmful behavior, it will have done its job.

It's been twenty-six years since I was a single mother, and I wasn't one for very long. My daughter, Jessica, was three months old when I separated from my former husband. She and I were alone for just a couple of years before I remarried and my current husband adopted her. But those years alone forged my relationship with her and forever changed the way I think about parenting and families.

When I began to write this book, I reproduced an old black-and-white picture of Jessica and me from that time together. An eight-by-ten-inch photo of me as a young, long-haired woman holding her round and smiling baby dons the cover of the three-ring binder that holds my notes. In this picture, my hand is wrapped around Jessica's wrist. I hold her hand close to my heart. Her little fingers are clutching mine. My albums are filled with photographs of us striking this same pose again and again. I was young, usually happy, often scared, sometimes lonely, and always broke. But that grip was constant and instinctive, a symbol of the fierce protectiveness I suspect I share with those of you who are reading this book.

The poet Muriel Rukeyser wrote that "The universe is made of stories, not of atoms." Although my time as a single parent was relatively brief, I am lucky enough to know many other single mothers who had many more years alone with their children. Some are grandmothers now; some have toddlers; others are getting ready to become mothers. My friends opened their hearts and lives to me and put me in touch with other single mothers who did the same. Their insights and commitment to help other single mothers shaped this book, and I remain in their debt for the assistance they've given me.

We learn best through stories. Women throughout the country, from most walks of life, share their wisdom and their stories throughout the pages of this book. They tell you what worked for them, and they tell you where they failed. Some mothers now in the midst of parenting pose questions and concerns that you might be pondering yourself. I can give you tools and information. The voices of those who weave the pages of this book into a rich and complete tapestry can give you pictures. Their stories breathe life into my text and add reason to my words. Grown-up sons and daughters who lived in single mother households at some point in their lives tell their stories here as well. Their words are insightful, sometimes painful, sometimes funny, but always honest.

Parents just want their children to grow up safe, healthy, happy, and relatively unscathed by the hard lessons of life. The adult sons and daughters of single mothers who speak throughout this book are testament that children who are loved and guided by caring adults in a nurturing community can indeed emerge as strong, sensitive, and happy men and women. Many have now gone forward to launch their own children. I was struck time and time again at how wise these young people are, and I was delighted by the respect, love, and deep gratitude they expressed for the mothers who raised them. Their words are affirmation and hope for single mothers who may often feel hopeless.

This is not a child-care manual, in the what-to-do-if-your-child-has-colic sense. The focus of this book is on how to take the best care of yourself so you will be better prepared to handle colic or other parenting challenges when they arise. It's often hard for busy moms to tend to their own needs, but taking care of yourself is like damming a river for power production. In times of drought, the river flows slowly or not at all. A dam collects the water and creates an energy reserve so power can be tapped as it is needed. This is what self-care is all about. When we take good care of ourselves, we create a reservoir of energy, patience, and love that will be there when we need it.

Much of this book is about how to nurture and nourish yourself, how to breathe deeply, slow down, and explore ways to carve out more time for yourself, which will ultimately enrich the time you have with your children. At the end of some sections of the book, readers are encouraged to "Take a Minute" to answer the questions posed, do the exercise suggested, or reflect on an idea that has been presented.

This book is also about asking for help. I still remember getting up early, packing Jessica's diaper bag and my things, bundling her up, and then buckling her into the infant seat I had strapped to the back of my yellow, ten-speed bicycle. We'd ride the three miles to Shirley's house; Shirley was the woman who took care of Jessica. Then I'd go across the street to my parents' house and shower and change before catching the bus to my downtown secretarial job. It exhausts me now to think of those days, but at the time I remember feeling so blessed to have a Shirley, to have supportive parents. I even felt lucky to have the yellow bike my friends had given me.

We do not parent in isolation. As cliché as the African saying has become, it really does "take a village to raise a child." Jessica was raised in a community of loving friends and family. She had many "surrogate parents," and now, as an adult, she maintains her own independent relationships with many of these people. It was an important step in the right direction when support groups started calling what happened at their meetings "mutual help" instead of "self-help." If there is one thing the many millions of people who belong to these groups all over the world have learned, it is the importance of asking for and giving help when it is needed. One of the goals of this book is to help you expand the circles of support you have in place and to guide you in creating support systems and networks if none currently exist. I have included a list of helpful organizations, books, and Web sites at the end of the book.

We don't stop being moms when our children grow up and move out of our homes. A host of new challenges and opportunities await the "empty-nesting single mother." This book will also discuss creative ways to embrace and celebrate the new relationships that can be formed with mature children and their partners. It will also talk about the joys of grandparenting and how the lessons learned as a single mother can be used in the role of grandmother.

Someone said that words are merely fingers pointing. I think that's true. I can string words and sentences together into ideas and paragraphs that might stimulate, direct, and even entertain. I can offer resources and reason, but I do not know exactly where or how the words will ultimately land. It is my deep hope that they fall softly and keep you warm.

ONE

Redefining Family

> If the family were a boat, it would be a canoe that makes no progress unless everyone paddles.
>
> If the family were a sport, it would be baseball: a long, slow, nonviolent game that is never over until the last out.
>
> If the family were a building, it would be an old, but solid structure that contains human history, and appeals to those who see the carved moldings under all the plaster, the wide plank floors under the linoleum, the possibilities.
>
> —From *Family Politics: Love and Power on an Intimate Frontier* by Letty Cottin Pogrebin

CREATING NEW IMAGES

If you asked me to draw a house right now, I'd draw the same house I drew when I was a little girl. A straight line would extend from left to right, connecting to the triangle that forms my roof, connecting it to the vertical lines that reach down to complete my boxy building. A little chimney would top the roof, emitting corkscrew smoke no matter what the season.

This has been my image of "house" for over forty-five years. No igloo, no hut, no mansion with a carriage house, and no apartment come to mind when I am asked to draw a house, although those structures are certainly home for a great many people. Only this one childish image is locked in my adult brain.

Many of us cling to old and outdated ideas of "family" in the same way I hold on to my childhood picture of "house." For many Americans, the word "family" conjures up the images that have been given to us our whole lives: a white, middle-class father who goes to work in a suit; his white, trim, and tireless wife who doesn't work outside the house so she can keep their suburban home immaculate; well-behaved children (one boy, one girl) fed and happy; and a dog (collie or cocker spaniel), perfectly groomed. As Bonnie Erbe wrote in the October 21, 1990, *Saint Paul Pioneer Press,* that "traditional" idea of family "is so close to extinction, it has a display case waiting for it in the Smithsonian, alongside the dodo bird."

If "traditional family" means a father who works, a mother who stays at home, and their children, a 1998 U.S. Bureau of the Census update reports that more than 70 percent of American families are not traditional. Most parents—single or married—work outside the home, and almost 28 percent of the family households in the United States are headed by a single parent with children under the age of eighteen. In fact, according to the Parents without Partners Web site, the 1990 U.S. Bureau of the Census estimated that as many as 61 percent of all children in the United States will spend all or part of their formative years in a single-parent household.

It is also interesting and, I think, significant to note that births to unwed mothers hit an all-time high in 1998. According to the National Center for Health Statistics, almost one-third of the babies born in 1998 were to unmarried women. Unlike the early 1990s, this is not a case of babies having babies, as was the concern then. In fact, the rate of teen births declined 18 percent between 1991 and 1998 but rose for women in their twenties and thirties during that same time period. What this report means is that more women are having babies, and an increasing number of women in their twenties and thirties are having children outside of marriage. The chief author of the abovementioned government report and other researchers say these figures indicate that society is becoming more accepting of unwed mothers.

Society is changing, and families are changing with it. My drawing of a house does not mirror the reality of what a house is any more than the myth of family mirrors the reality of what a family actually is. Yet many of us believe the myth of what a family *should be,* and if our family doesn't look like that mythical picture, we think that something is wrong with us or that we have somehow shortchanged our children by not giving them the whole family package: mom, dad, siblings, a house, and financial security.

> My son is going to be thirty soon, and I was going through some old photos and things for his surprise party. I came across a box I had saved of his kindergarten schoolwork, and in it was a "Poster of Myself," on which he had printed, in uneven lines and pinched letters, his three wishes: (1) a puppy, (2) a kitty named Sammy, and (3) a daddy to live with me. His father was an abusive jerk, and I have no regrets about divorcing him, but there I was, twenty-five years later, still able to cry over my son's pencil list of wishes.*

Contemporary families come in all shapes and sizes. There are married couples with children; married couples without children; single mothers with children; single fathers with children; unmarried couples with children; gay and lesbian parents with children; and grandparents, aunts, and uncles raising children.

---

* Indented text throughout this book represents the words of others: current and former single mothers, adult children who lived for some period of time in a single mother household, or professionals who work with single-parent families. These persons are presented anonymously to protect the privacy of those involved, and in some cases minor details have been changed to ensure anonymity.

I was always aware growing up that families come in many variations. My parents had friends who had families that were multiracial, same-sex partners raising children, parents with different religions, etc., so I always have had a pretty liberal attitude about what a "family" consists of. My perceptions haven't changed since becoming a single mother.

Creating new images of family can be exhilarating. As single mothers replace old pictures with new ones that more accurately capture their own imperfect, wonderfully diverse, and very real families, they change the black-and-white 1950s television shows that play like memories in our minds into a new Technicolor movie. Single mothers can title this new movie *A Real Family* and cast themselves and their children in the starring roles.

Take a Minute

The Metaphorical Family

In the excerpt from her book at the beginning of this chapter, Letty Cottin Pogrebin creates wonderful metaphors for family. In her words, family becomes a canoe, a baseball game.

A metaphor is a figure of speech that compares two unlike things in a fresh way. Metaphors can help break us out of old ways of thinking. When we use metaphors, we can make new connections that shake the dust off our old definitions so we can create new meanings that are closer to our own life experience. Clouds were not just clouds to the poet Pablo Neruda, for example. Through metaphor he turned them into "white handkerchiefs of goodbye," to reflect the loss he was feeling on that particular day.

Take a minute and make a list of all the different images you associate with family—not the fairy-tale family you've been told to believe in, but *real* family, your family. My list would look like this:

Family is:

- the laughter of children
- wind chimes, some days crashing loudly against each other; other days balanced and still
- a river of experience flowing to an ocean of possibility
- the hearts of friends, beating in unison
- love, unconditional; help without asking
- a mirror
- a blanket that keeps me warm and protected
- a garden of love, diverse flowers blooming wildly
- a tapestry stitched together with stories
- a work in progress

My metaphors give a color, texture, and movement to the idea of family that helps me think about my own family in a different, nontraditional way. Now I am freer to fashion my own definition of family.

Create your own list of metaphors for family. Is your image of what a family looks like changing?

FAMILY HISTORY

I still remember the day my own family was "de-mythified." I was in my mid-thirties, having coffee with my Grandma Reeck in her comfortable little kitchen on Cherokee Street. Gram and her kitchen had been a sanctuary for Jessica and me after my separation and divorce. The geraniums on the windowsills, the sturdy chrome-legged table that was always covered with a fresh, pressed cloth, and the smell of chocolate-chip cookies were a welcome refuge. Visiting Gram was like taking a warm, two-hour bath.

"You never judged me, Gram," I said on that summer day thirty years ago. "Here I was, alone with a three-month-old baby, and you never once questioned my decision."

"I couldn't stand to see how bad he treated you," my grandmother told me. Then she leaned toward me conspiratorially and said in a hushed voice, even though we were the only two people in the room, "You know, Ma was divorced."

The family secret was out. My great-grandmother Nettie, who had ten children in fifteen years on the farm in Trimbelle, Wisconsin, had become a single mother when several of her children were still in their teens. "You never talked about divorce in those days," Gram said. "But it happened then too."

In her book *The Way We Never Were,* Stephanie Coontz likens what's happened to our perception of family to the way children recount their summer vacations. She says that when students are first asked to make a list of the good things and the bad things about their summer, the lists are about equal. If the exercise is repeated later in the school year, however, the good list grows and the bad becomes shorter. By the end of the year, the bad memories have faded so much, the children describe idealized vacations, not the real ones that were a mixture of positive and negative experiences. This is, she says, what happens to families. Over the years, the negatives fade and we're left with images of the *Leave It to Beaver* families of the 1950s.

If we take a closer look at families throughout American history, however, we find that there has never been one static picture that fit all families and that there are reasons that families today don't look exactly like families of two centuries ago.

One of the reasons we have higher divorce rates today is because people now live longer. Marriages didn't last all that long two hundred years ago either, but it was death not divorce that ended them. As Coontz reminds us, one-third to one-half of Colonial children lost at least one parent to death by the time the children were twenty-one years old.

Things may have been better for wealthy Victorian families who come closer to the idealized picture of family, with the husband going off to work while the mother stayed home with the children, but the poorer families of that era did not live the lives of characters in a Jane Austen novel. They were the ones who worked as servants, cleaning the houses and watching the children of their more prosperous employers. According to Coontz, the nineteenth century was rife with child labor problems and poor working conditions. Newspapers from the mid-1800s told of factories where half the workers were children under the age of eleven. As is true throughout history, women and children bore the brunt of poverty.

The Great Depression pulled families together and tore them apart, as a crisis often does. In some families, parents and children worked in close harmony to survive economic hardships; in others, out-of-work fathers became isolated or violent, women got exhausted trying to hold things together, and children grew angry because they had to quit school and get jobs to support the family. Then came World War II when many mothers went to work and raised their children alone while their husbands went overseas to fight. My mother still talks of those years with a mixture of pride and pain. My brother was just a toddler, and my sister was born while my dad fought in Germany. Mom worked hard and budgeted her ration coupons and, with the help of my grandparents, kept her little family safe.

When husbands and fathers came home from World War II, responsibilities shifted again in American families. Many women who had joined the labor force during the war turned their jobs back over to the men they had replaced. The post-war economic boom encouraged consumer spending, and new government programs provided housing, education, and job opportunities for many who struggled before the war. Divorce rates went down and birth rates went up. Television sitcoms that equated life with family were born. On the surface, American families appeared to be flourishing.

But scratch beneath that surface, and we uncover some interesting facts. The prosperous middle-class America of the 1950s that we celebrate nostalgically was, for the most part, white America. Minorities were noticeably absent from the privileges enjoyed by the families we saw on television. Food stamps and public housing assistance were not yet available, so the poor had little recourse. Most older people had no medical insurance, and only half the population had savings.

All was not as rosy at it seemed for the middle class or even the wealthy. Coontz quotes a mother of a colleague who refers to her life in the 1950s as the four Bs: booze, bowling, bridge, and boredom. She says that when *McCall's* ran an article in 1956 entitled "The Mother Who Ran Away," the magazine's readership skyrocketed. Tranquilizers were developed in the 1950s, and doctors increasingly prescribed them for their unhappy female patients. Women's drinking also increased. Teen pregnancies increased dramatically, but illegitimate births were often hidden when the teen parents married or the young mother remained in her parents' home.

When we fast-forward in time, through the era of civil rights, through all the political and social upheaval of the 1960s and 1970s, through the sexual revolution, the women's movement, the self-help movement, through all the other individual, family, and societal changes, we discover that family *values*— our concern for children, the importance of kinship and community, the desire to provide a secure and safe environment for those we love—have not changed all that much. What has changed is the way people choose to live with each other.

For a single mom, family is more encompassing than just relatives. I remember having to rely on friends and neighbors a lot to help me out. It sounds kind of hokey to bring up the "it takes a village to raise a child" thing, but it holds true for single moms. Whether it was baby-sitting or giving rides or helping with Boy Scout badges, my family grew to include neighbors and friends. Even though I'm not a single mom anymore, we live far away from all our relatives. So even though we have a two-parent household, I still think of our friends and neighbors as part of our family. They are witness to more of my children's lives than any blood relatives. They fill in for family when they come to our kids' sporting events, school plays, birthdays.

TAKE A MINUTE

Revisiting History

The messages we receive from our grandparents and parents are powerful and long lasting. For the longest time I believed that my brother and I were the only ones in my family of origin who got divorced. That belief helped fuel the myth in my family that marriage was forever and that family meant a mother and father and their children. When I got divorced, I felt like I was breaking a family rule as well as a societal rule.

My beliefs shifted when I found out my great-grandmother had been divorced. When I learned a little more about marriage and family throughout American history, things shifted even more. It was like looking through a kaleidoscope. All the jumbled pieces settled into a clearer pattern, and I was merely one piece of the pattern, not some disconnected fragment that didn't fit into the overall design.

Take a minute and think about the messages you've received about family from your parents and grandparents, from television shows, from movies and books, and from the world around you. How have these messages affected how you think about yourself as a single mother? What messages about family do you want to deliver to your children?

THE POWER OF MYTH

> "Once upon a time . . ." "In a long-ago time, in a faraway
> land . . ." "They lived happily ever after."

We live with and by our stories. Stories teach us, scare us,
stimulate us into action, connect us to each other, and entertain
us. Myths and stories can shape the way we think about something. They plant such powerful pictures in our minds that,
over time, we mistake the invented images for mirrors. Without even realizing it, we see ourselves as the mythical figure
and begin to expect the mythical outcome. Like the heroes and
heroines of our favorite fairy tales, we imagine that if we are
kind and helpful and good of heart, we will find the person of
our dreams, fall in love, and live happily ever after with our
partner and our children.

If these expectations are not met, it is sometimes easier to
find fault with ourselves than to let go of the myth we've
grown up with. At such times, it is not uncommon for the "if
onlys" to kick in: "If only I had tried harder. If only I were
smarter, richer, funnier, prettier, more patient . . ."

While the notions of what an idealized family should be
might work in fairy tales, they are impractical when it comes
to the complexities of our real lives. When reality comes in
conflict with long-held beliefs, we are too often left with guilt
(feeling bad about what we do) or shame (feeling bad about
who we are).

> When I lived with my mom, all my other friends had
> both a mom and a dad, so I felt different, like they were
> better than me. But I know now that wasn't true at all. I
> haven't ever lived in a "normal" household, but I realize
> you don't really need a normal household; you just need
> people who love you and are supportive.

A myth that enlightens is useful; a myth that enslaves can
be tragic.

I was too ashamed to tell anyone how bad my eleven-year marriage actually was. I didn't want anyone to know how much my husband drank. I didn't tell anyone how much I was growing to hate him, because it didn't seem right. My father was an alcoholic who treated my mother absolutely terribly. My life was sweet compared to hers, so I felt that if she could withstand such treatment, I should just "deal with it." When you keep all these things to yourself for years, your decision to get out of the relationship appears "sudden" to everyone else. My perception at that time was that most people thought I was making up things and that "it wasn't really that bad." His parents, who up until then had been wonderful in-laws, decided I was rotten and he was the victim. Apparently being nice to the children would show support for me; therefore, the girls weren't accepted either.

The "happy endings" to these types of stories came only after the women let go of the myth that family had to be a mom, a dad, and the children they conceived together.

Take a Minute

Inventing New Myths

One way to let go of unrealistic myths is to become the author of your own life story.

Take a minute and think about your life. Close your eyes and picture yourself, a strong and intelligent woman, a protective mother, a worthy human being. Envision yourself standing straight and proud with your children. All of you are smiling. Beneath this picture is the caption "My family."

Now take another minute and create your own myth. Write down the words "Once upon a time," and go from there. Be bold. Give yourself credit where credit is due. Celebrate your courage. Write yourself a happy ending.

Here's my story:

Once upon a time there was a young woman named Cynthia. One day she met a boy, and they dated for three years. They thought they loved each other, and they got married, but they didn't live happily ever after. Some nights, the loneliness was so heavy she would quietly cry herself to sleep, careful not to wake him. This went on for three more years.

And then something wonderful happened. Cynthia felt the stirring of life inside her and knew that she would be a mother soon. Tom was not happy about this surprise, and his verbal taunting became crueler, his emotional battering more hateful.

But something had changed in Cynthia, and she went about with a newfound and fierce determination, readying herself and her life for the arrival of her daughter. She vowed to protect her and to raise her in an environment of love and peace.

So when Jessica was born, they left Tom and the dark house. The two of them were a family, and they lived happily ever after with their cat Antoinette and their faithful dog Maxine.

COMBATING STEREOTYPES

When we accept as gospel the belief that the ideal family consists of a father, a mother, and their children, we feed the negative stereotypes that are directed toward those who don't conform to that ideal. We may feel less than, not as good as, or different from those who do live with their children in a two-parent heterosexual relationship.

> When my son was in first grade, his school had a family day. Each student got points for the family members who attended. I came with my ex-husband's mother, but only fathers and mothers and sisters and brothers counted as family, so my son only got one point—for me. He was heartbroken and embarrassed. The message those nuns sent was powerful and hurtful: *your* family doesn't count as much as *their* families; in fact, you aren't a real family at all. I took him out of that school as soon as I could.

Self-esteem and success are integrally related to how we are perceived by those around us. It is human nature to rise to positive expectations or sink to negative expectations. If we approach the world apologetically, we also risk having our children pick up on our attitudes. If children aren't expected to do as well in school because they come from a "broken" or "abnormal" home, they might not do as well. Their poor performance then becomes a self-fulfilling prophecy.

Stephanie Coontz writes that one review of literature on single-parent families found that the only situations in which children of one-parent families suffered losses of self-esteem were those in which the families were stigmatized. She points to the example of teachers who, when shown a videotape of a child engaging in a variety of actions, consistently rated the child more negatively if they were first told the child came from a divorced family than they did if they assumed the child lived with two parents.

> I hate the stereotyping directed at my son. If he is shy, it *must* be because there are no men in his life. If he throws a temper tantrum or cries, it *must* be because there are no men in his life. It gets old, especially when these assumptions are made without getting to know us.

Well-meaning people can undermine your and your children's abilities with negative expectations and assumptions, however subtle their comments may be. Sometimes the persons making the assumptions may not even realize how detrimental their attitudes can be. After all, they grew up with the same myths about families that we did. But each time your child's teacher "tsk tsks" about your "situation," or a boss, coworker, friend, or relative talks about broken homes or those poor kids without a father, you and your children are being exposed to negative stereotypes.

> When I tell some people that I am a single mom, some look at me with a look of sympathy or pity. I don't want people to feel sorry for me or judge me without knowing anything about the circumstances. I don't judge others, and I don't want them judging me. I am proud that my daughter and I have a better life now alone than I would have ever had had I stayed married.

If single mothers and their children are led to believe they are less able to succeed in school, at work, or in life than those who live in a two-parent home, they might not do as well because the stage is set for failure. Researchers like Claude M. Steele have also determined that just the threat of being prejudged on the basis of some negative stereotype can undermine a person's ability to succeed. They have found that even people with high self-esteem who aren't victims of negative stereotypes react to what Steele calls "stereotype threat."* For example, when white male students who were strong in math were given a math test and told it was one on which Asians usually did better, they performed worse than the white male students of equal ability who had not heard this comment. In other words, it doesn't matter how competent the individual or how false the statement; just the mere suggestion that someone is not expected to succeed as well as someone else can lead to underachievement.

While we can't hope to easily change societal stereotypes about single-parent families that have been in place for centuries, we can help shift attitudes in our communities and workplaces. Steele and his research colleagues were able to improve the overall grades of black students at a racially mixed Michigan university when they developed an integrated "living and learning" community where students could meet to talk about the personal side of college life. The researchers speculate that when members of one racial group hear members of another racial group expressing the same doubts and concerns they have, the threat of racial stereotype is lessened.

In much the same way, we can lessen the threat of stereotypes about single-parent families when we get to know people in our work and home communities on a personal basis. The writer Mary Karr defines a dysfunctional family as "any family with more than one person in it." We are all human beings joined together in our imperfection. When we start seeing each other as individuals who share the same concerns about home repairs and school schedules and finances and the weather; when we start seeing each other as devoted parents who want to see their children safe and happy, we can begin to get beyond titles, beyond labels, and yes, even beyond stereotypes.

---

*For a thorough discussion on "stereotype threat," see Claude M. Steele, "Thin Ice: 'Stereotype Threat' and Black College Students," *The Atlantic Monthly,* August 1999, 44–54.

TAKE A MINUTE

Moving Beyond Stereotypes

Attitude shifts begin at home. We can't expect others to accept single mother families as *real* families if we view them as abnormal or as "families in waiting"—as if they aren't really families now but could be if Mom would only find herself a partner.

One easy way to practice changing attitudes is to think of two positives for every negative thought you have about something. *Take a minute* and quickly list some negative things you've heard, read, or thought about single-parent families. Across from each negative statement, write two positive statements that reflect your own experience, your own reality. Such a list might read:

Belief	Reality
1. Children from single-parent homes have difficulty in school.	• My daughter made the honor roll.
	• Sheila's son is captain of the ski team.
2. Children who grow up without a father have emotional problems.	• My children have strong male role models in their lives.
	• My children are well-adjusted and happy.
3. Single mothers can't give their children what two-parent families can.	• I have uninterrupted quality time with my children.
	• My kids and I are a team; we work together to keep things going.

Belief	Reality
4. Single-parent homes are sad and serious.	• Our home is filled with laughter. • There is so much joy and so much less tension since the divorce.

Now read over your list. Do you feel your attitudes shifting?

CREATING A WORKING DEFINITION
OF FAMILY

By now you should have a pretty good idea of what "family" means to you and your children. Your definition of family might differ from your neighbor's definition or your mother's definition or your friend's definition, and that's just fine because your family might not look like your neighbor's family or your friend's family or your family of origin.

> I used to think that "family" was first and foremost those to whom one is related by blood or law, but divorce finished off that point of view. And the enormous amount of assistance that I received from extended family during my parenting clinched the feeling. At my daughter's wedding, her toast was "to all my mothers." Now I think of "family" as all those who self-consciously take responsibility for each other, in good times and bad.

Your concept of family may be more fluid, changing a little with each life experience. This is the case for a soon-to-be-married single mom who grew up in a single mother household:

> My perception of family is constantly being refined. I think because I was part of what everyone considered a "broken" family, I never felt like mine was legitimate. Growing up, family simply meant the people related to me. Later, I realized that my mom, sister, and I made up a family unit. Now, as I've come to better understand the importance and meaning of family, my definition has expanded to include my baby, my fiancé's family, and other members of my extended family.

For other single mothers, family is a verb—a cooperative process that requires active involvement:

I tell the kids that they have two families now: one with their dad and one with me. Our family is a team that values all players; where everyone gets opportunities to win; a safe place where all feelings are valid and openly on the table; where members work together to find good ways of expressing those feelings. All those things are key to having family that works and stays together and grows with everybody. That's what I think these days, but it may change six months from now, as I continue to "grow up."

While new definitions of family do not require the traditional idea of marriage, they still include a strong sense of commitment:

A family is a group of people (adults and/or children) who love and care about one another and who foster a sense of connection in day-to-day living. This transcends biological and marital relationships. It's the group you can count on to provide unconditional love and support. I no longer think it can be defined by titles.

Unconditional love. Open communication. Those who self-consciously take care of each other in good times and bad. A bond that transcends biology or marriage. A team that values its members. A safe place in which to feel and express a range of emotions. People who share a strong daily connection. An organic relationship that changes with the experiences and growth of its members. This is how some single mothers have come to view "family." It is such a rich and positive list, inclusive and absent of judgment. What child would not thrive in an environment that embraced these qualities?

One of the most valuable gifts single mothers can give themselves and their children is the belief that they are a real family. Even if the family you had yesterday doesn't look exactly like the family you have today, you are still family. You know this is true because you are living this truth.

TAKE A MINUTE

Defining Family

There is such power in words, in names, in titles. The childhood chant "Sticks and stones can break my bones but words can never hurt me" is a lie, and we do a disservice if we teach that to our children. Words can hurt you. It makes a difference what words we use to describe ourselves and others.

Words are like clay: their meanings can be shaped and smoothed until we create the sculpture that suits us best. As we have seen, the definition of family changes from person to person, from experience to experience.

Take a minute and reclaim the word "family." Shape it to fit your life, your relationships, your reality. Start with the phrase "Family is . . ." and complete your own definition. Write it down. Tape it to your refrigerator, bedroom mirror, or computer. Discuss it with your children if they are old enough for such discussion. Get their input, and create a combined definition if they have more ideas. This is your working definition of family, the torch you light to view the world of relationships.

If you have young children, you may want to talk about what family means to them and then look for pictures in magazines that capture the images and concepts you come up with. Remember the metaphor discussion—the images don't have to be of people; they can be colorful designs, nature images, or pictures that represent the feelings or atmosphere of what "family" means to you and your children. Cut these pictures out and make a collaborative family collage to hang up where you can all admire your creation, your family.

TWO

Creating Community

◉　◉　◉

We thrive best in the company of others. We evolved while living in small, sustainable communities that shared in raising children, growing food, building shelter, designing work, making crafts, worshipping and celebrating. This is our social-genetic inheritance, passed down as surely as the color of our skin and eyes.

—From *Calling the Circle: The First and Future Culture* by Christina Baldwin

SEEKING AND RECEIVING SUPPORT

Did you hear the one about the guy in the flood? As the rain came day after day, the river on which his house was located rose higher and higher until the authorities finally gave the word to evacuate. Neighbor after neighbor packed their belongings and left their homes, but the man refused to go with them. "God will take care of me," he told them confidently when they begged him to leave. "I'll just stay here and pray. I'm sure God will save me." The water rose higher, rushing into the first floor of the house. Undaunted, the man went to his second-story bedroom to pray some more. When the sheriff came by in a boat directing him to leave, the stubborn man shouted from his second-story window, "Thank you, but I'm going to stay. God will take care of me." And still the river kept rising, finally forcing the man to seek refuge on his rooftop. As he sat on his roof praying, a helicopter flew overhead, dangling a rope ladder for the man to climb. But the stubborn man waved the helicopter away, shouting, "I'll be okay. God will take care of me." But the river was more stubborn than the man, and it rose high enough to swallow both the house and the man who still sat praying upon the roof. He was a little miffed when he got to heaven. "God, I prayed and prayed. Why didn't you save me?" God, looking just a tad impatient, answered, "I sent the sheriff, a boat, and a helicopter. What more did you expect?"

Sometimes we're like the stubborn man. We get so distracted waiting for help to arrive that we don't notice when it's right before our eyes. Our pride, fear, uncertainty, or just plain exhaustion can overwhelm us and keep us isolated on our own rooftops. But if we reach out and embrace the hands that are extended to us, wonderful things can happen. Community can happen.

> When my husband moved out two years ago, our big old fixer-up-house was under construction. My daughter was just a toddler, and I worked full-time. We were fairly new to the neighborhood, and I felt totally overwhelmed at all there was to do. One of my neighbors got wind of what was going on, and one Saturday a dozen neighbors just showed up, tools and materials in hand, ready to tackle the house renovation. "We want you to be able to stay here," they told me when I tried to protest. There was no arguing them out of this, and they worked for weeks until the project was completed. They were like a little Habitat for Humanity group. They made me believe that we'd be all right, that we could do this.

> Unlike the man on the roof, this woman had the graciousness to accept the help that was offered—no easy task for a

single mom who is trying to convince herself and others that she can "handle it," whatever "it" might be.

When my husband and I separated, I was pregnant with our second child and had to move in with my parents. It was hard to accept help, but my sister reminded me of all the times I've helped others through difficult times. I found out others feel good about being able to help.

When we care for each other's children, we are practicing what psychologist Erik Erikson called an act of "generativity"—we are helping to guide the next generation safely into adulthood. Erikson viewed generativity as a reciprocal and instinctive act because humans need to be needed, and we grow into more complete beings when we have someone to care for.

There were two elderly sisters who lived across the street from us. They treated my kids like their grandchildren, offering them their time for stories, treats, chores, etc. I was going to school at the time and my daughter got the flu during my finals. The sisters came over to my apartment to baby-sit even though they ran the risk of getting the flu themselves.

When help doesn't just come our way, it is necessary to actively seek it, a frightening prospect for those of us who are more used to giving help than getting it. I remember having to call my parents at midnight one night when Jessica awoke with a high fever and I was frantic with worry. Plus I felt like I was flunking Motherhood 101. Nothing I tried would bring her temperature down to normal, and after my third conversation with the pediatrician on call, I was told to bring her to the hospital. I knew something was terribly wrong, and I was so relieved when my parents came immediately with no questions or eye-rolling statements like "You're probably just overreacting." Jessica was diagnosed with septicemia—bacteria in her bloodstream—and hospitalized in isolation for over a week. It tore my heart to leave my nine-month-old baby in a hospital with strangers, no matter how caring, but with the help of my parents, I made it through that terrifying ordeal.

No one is born knowing how to parent. It's a continuing education course with inconsistent patterns and ever-changing answers, because we and our children are always growing, always changing. We need information, direction, consolation, and understanding. Sometimes we just need a distraction. But it's difficult to ask for help. Too frequently we feel we have no right to bother anyone with mundane or ordinary concerns, that only crises earn assistance.

> I never felt that my needs should come before the children's, and when I chose to do something like going out on the weekend, I always felt guilty. I didn't like to ask my mother to watch the kids too much because she never went out a weekend in her life that I can remember. My sister who lived close was also a single mom, struggling with the same problems that I had. I certainly couldn't ask her to take care of my children. I did have one ex-sister-in-law who lived close and who knew everything about me and my marriage, and she helped whenever she could. I also had a neighbor who was a new single mom who did not handle her situation at all well. She fell into depression and needed much more support from me than I did from her. Actually, helping her made me a stronger person.

Charles Dickson, a North Carolina clergyman and chemistry instructor, urges us to take some lessons from the geese when it comes to living in community. He writes that whenever a goose falls out of the flock's V formation, it suddenly feels the drag and resistance of trying to fly alone, so it quickly learns to get back into formation to take advantage of the lifting power of the bird in front of it. By flying together this way, the whole flock can fly much farther. "If we have as much sense as the geese, we will be willing to accept help when we need it as well as lend help to others when they need it," writes Dickson.

There are three basic steps in asking for help. The first step is to identify your problem, need, or fear. Often just naming a pain or difficulty is a release because by doing so, you give yourself permission to be vulnerable, to be less than perfect. Even Batman had to be Bruce Wayne once in a while, and when he *was* Batman, he had his trusty sidekick Robin beside him to get him out of scrapes. You can't be Supermom twenty-four hours a day, seven days a week either. You need to get some sidekicks in place.

> I remember when my kids were little and I had a terrible migraine headache. It was so bad I lay in bed in pain, crying, with the curtains drawn and the door shut. Even the pillow hurt my head. I could not deal with my kids and yelled at them if they opened the door or made any noise. I felt like I should go to the emergency room, but I could not drive myself and leave my children alone. I didn't know who to ask for help, so I didn't ask anyone and suffered through it. It was hard.

After you've got a pretty good idea why you need help, the second step is to figure out who can most appropriately give you the help you need. This is an imperfect process, and you cannot predict the responses you'll receive. Some people may disappoint you by not being readily available, and others will totally surprise you by their willingness to come to your aid. It is a good idea to think about the different aspects of your life and your children's lives and brainstorm a list of people or organizations you could contact if a need arose in a particular area. The friend you'd call to fix your car may be different from the one you'd call to take care of your children if you run unexpectedly late from work. Sometimes the seriousness of a problem will dictate whom you will call. You might call your sister to get advice about your son's sniffles, but you'd probably call your family doctor if he had a bronchial cough and fever.

> As a single parent, I rely a lot on my friends who have raised their children and can give me parenting advice. I know other single mothers who I call and talk to when I'm having difficulties. When my children were small, I joined a Parents Anonymous support group, and it was helpful. My employers have been wonderful about being flexible with my working hours so that if I have a sick child, I can leave work and make up the time another day.

The third step is to actually ask for the help you need. To ask for help is to practice humility, a noble virtue. Philosopher Simone Weil called humility "compassion directed at oneself." You are worthy of tenderness, and you are entitled to compassion from others and from yourself.

It is important to be as specific and clear as you can be in your request for assistance. And if people aren't able to help you, it is good practice to accept their answer at face value. They might have other commitments or they might not be able to help for some complicated and personal reasons you are not aware of. Think about the times a favor has been asked of you and the times you have not been able to do that favor for whatever reason. If one person can't help you, say thanks anyway, and call another person. If that person can't help, think about an organization or professional you could turn to.

> I've been in Al-Anon for about two years, and my group gives me space to explore my options and responsibilities. They don't give me advice. I've been able to make tough decisions, bear a lot of pain, and focus on growing myself. And we've had a lot of good laughs. I don't always "get" the program, but it's progress, not perfection. My church has had great single-parenting programs

that I really enjoy and appreciate. During my divorce, I used a women's counseling service, as well as my therapist and my chiropractor.

There are many national organizations for single parents that have local subsidiaries. The National Organization of Single Mothers (704-888-KIDS) and Parents without Partners (800-637-7974) are just a couple of many options. A good place to start is to contact your local United Way and ask for their First Call for Help directory, which is updated every year or two. County social service agencies, community centers, local churches, and community education offices are also good resources. A list of other resources can be found at the end of this book (page 168).

It's a good idea to compile your resource list during a period of relative calm so you will have names and numbers at your fingertips when you need them in a hurry. Don't wait until the pipe breaks, the dog runs away, your child gets sick, or a relationship is in shambles to get a support network in place. Approach this task like a detective, uncovering clues and leads over time. Ask people at your children's school, your workplace, your grocery store, or your church for ideas and information.

I teach kindergarten, first, and second grade in Florida, and many of my students are from single-parent or single-grandparent homes. Single mothers need to know they certainly are not alone in their family situations, and the burdens they face are faced by many others like them. The number of children from single-parent homes has increased gradually over the eighteen years I have taught, and now single-parent families are as common as two-parent families. A one-parent family has just as much potential for success as a two-parent family if single mothers seek help and support from others when it is needed. It is important for those who work with single mothers to be sensitive to the time issues and financial burdens single-parent families face. Schools need to be flexible enough to adjust scheduling of conferences and school functions to accommodate the working schedules of parents. Classroom teachers need to be inclusive of all family situations and to assure children that each family is equally important regardless of its makeup. The best situations for children are ones in which everyone works together to make them comfortable and happy.

People like this elementary teacher love to share knowledge and resources. Let them help you.

Take a Minute

Listing Your Resources

Listing can give you a survey of what is available. It's a way
to break down an often overwhelming whole into manageable parts. A list can be a summary of what you need, a summary of what you want, a summary of what you have, or an
idea of what you can do to get your needs met. A list is easy
to add to and easy to alter as your situation and needs
change. A list can also help you articulate your request for
help when you need to ask for assistance.

Take a minute and list the people you would call:

- to discuss a personal problem or fear
- for child care
- for health care advice for you and your children
- for health care emergencies
- for financial or legal help
- for automobile advice or repair
- for household maintenance or advice
- for last-minute scheduling changes or conflicts (e.g.,
  Who could pick up your children if you were at work
  and one of them became ill at school?)
- for scholastic advice or counseling for you or your
  children
- for spiritual advice or guidance
- for social interaction for you and your children
- to exercise or play
- for laughter or consolation when you're down in the
  dumps

Categorize your list in whatever way feels logical to you.
Include addresses and phone numbers, and add backup con-
tacts whenever you think of them. Let people know you're

compiling this network, and ask them if it's all right to contact them when a need arises. Negotiate with friends to see if there is anything you can do in exchange for their help. Be creative. Barter services. Help the teenager next door with his math if he'll mow your lawn. Weed your mother's garden in exchange for her watching your children. This is mutuality. This is community in action.

REDEFINING FRIENDSHIP

I was a single mother during the 1970s, during those days of peace, love, long hair, and bell-bottoms. I worked part-time and took classes at the University of Minnesota when I could afford them. My friends and I were hippies, drawn together by the politics and passions of the Vietnam era. We were a tribe, we were a clan, we were a family. Jessica and I lived by ourselves, but I always knew that help, support, and companionship were only a phone call away. No one had much money, so it was common to have community potluck dinners or picnics. We embraced each other as family and shared child-care responsibilities when we were together.

Although we certainly weren't conscious of it at the time, by operating at this tribal level, we were modeling community for each other and for our children. We abided by unspoken rules of friendship and community that incorporated certain expectations and boundaries. We were comforted and cared for, and we were expected to comfort and care in return.

Bonds were formed thirty years ago that remain intact today for both Jessica and me. My hair and my friends' hair is graying, our bodies are thickening, and our lives are middle class now, but our doors and hearts are still open to each other and to our children, some of whom have children of their own. In fact, as I write this, Jessica is packing her bags and her dog to go visit two of her surrogate parents in northern Minnesota.

It may not be as easy to create a cohesive community today as it was three decades ago in the tribal culture that existed then, but it's still possible.

> My women's group members all lived in the neighborhood, and we had an "open door, open dinner table, and open bed" policy about each other's children. When my father was dying, they took turns bringing dinner to my house every night for six weeks, put the children to bed, and stayed until I returned home. That's family.

In our book *New Life, New Friends,* Christina Baldwin and I defined friendship as "a mutual bond of respect, trust, and vulnerability that encourages healthy growth and acceptance." When you ask for support, you practice being vulnerable, one of the conditions of friendship. When you are vulnerable, you are giving your friend permission to be vulnerable too, and this is mutuality in action. It is a circle game.

Motherhood changes us, and our changes create changes in our relationships. Mothers can't be as spontaneous as they used to be. Their priorities and interests are different, they are more tired, they worry more, and they often explode with inexplicable pride and joy over the most basic accomplishments of their children. It might be hard for friends and relatives who don't have children to relate when you call them excitedly with news that Brandon has just gone to the bathroom in the big toilet for the first time, but if the friendship is solid, you and your friends will learn how to reconnect in this new phase of life and experience.

The best relationships are pliable ones that bend to accommodate change. Such accommodation is a practice in empathy: you want friends to be able to accept and understand who you are now, and you need to be ready to respond to how they feel about your changed relationship. As a woman and mother of worth, you need to surround yourself and your children with those who support and encourage your growth as an individual and as a mother—people who love you and your children and want you all to succeed.

Warning bells should go off if you feel deflated or shot down after a visit with someone. You owe it to yourself and to your children to be choosy. Sort out whom you want to be with and whom you want influencing your children, and work to nurture only the positive relationships that nurture you and your family. People change, and the changes aren't always parallel. That's okay. With more than five billion people on the planet, there are plenty of potential friends to choose from.

I've lost a few friends in my "divorce recovery," friends I'd known for years, but that happens when you change a lot. It may be for the best, although I have not found the friends yet to replace the hole that's left.

If you have doubts about a particular relationship, ask yourself:

- Does this person help you grow as a person and as a mother? How do you contribute to this person's growth?
- Does this person model healthy behavior to you and your children?
- Are there still benefits that you derive from the relationship? Is it worthwhile to stay in the relationship to reap those benefits?
- Do you and this person practice mutual respect? How?
- What interests do you and this person still have in common?
- How do your differences enhance or inhibit your growth?

Distancing yourself from friends or acquaintances with whom you feel tension or negativity can be difficult but may be necessary. (In the case of former husbands and their families, it may not be possible.) How you establish this distance depends on the degree of closeness you share with this individual. It may require no action on your part, or you may choose to express your concerns directly or in a letter in a clear and nonblaming way. You might discover that your friend has similar concerns, and the two of you may choose to work together to redefine your relationship.

TAKE A MINUTE

Negotiating Healthy Relationships

Years ago, a friend who was in recovery for drug abuse and alcohol abuse gave me a copy of "A Credo for My Relationship with Another" as a blueprint for our own relationship. I wish I knew whom to credit for these wise and practical sentiments, but I do not know who the author is.

Take a minute to read this adaptation. Hold the statements and intentions up to the mirror of your friendships and see if each relationship measures up to these standards. If you choose, share it with a friend as my friend did with me. Use it as a model or even a contract for your relationship with that person. If you want, you can make it official by each signing a copy.

A Credo for My Relationship with Another

Each of us is a separate person with our own unique needs and the right to try to meet those needs. Let's try to be genuinely accepting of each other when we are trying to meet our respective needs or when we are having problems meeting our needs.

When we share our problems with each other, let's try to listen to each other acceptingly and understandingly in a way that will facilitate our finding our own solutions rather than depending on each other for solutions. When we have a problem because the other's behavior is interfering with meeting our needs, let's tell each other openly and honestly how we are feeling. At those times, we will listen and may choose to modify our behavior.

At those times when neither of us can modify our behavior to meet the needs of the other, let us commit ourselves to resolving each such conflict without ever resorting to the use of either my power or yours to win at the expense of the other losing. Let us always search for solutions that will be acceptable to both of us. In this way, each of us can become what we are capable of being, and we can continue to relate to each other in mutual respect, friendship, love, and peace.

CREATING AN INTENTIONAL COMMUNITY

I often envy the immediate bond members of Alcoholics Anonymous seem to have. The "Honk If You Know Bill W." bumper stickers, the recovery medallions that sometimes slip from wallets or are attached to key chains, or the use of an AA slogan identify members to each other as part of the tribe. Maybe it would be easier for single moms to connect with each other if they had T-shirts or bumper stickers, but they are finding each other even without secret handshakes.

Through organizations and by themselves, more and more single mothers are discovering that they can create communities for themselves and their children where they can get emotional and practical support. One minister in Oakland, California, described how her parishioners pride themselves on their communal approach to child care after Sunday services. "We open our parish hall to everyone, and we all share in the job of watching the children. You usually can't tell what child goes with what parent because we're all one big family for that hour each week. Parents get a little break, and we all get to know the kids a bit better."

In the Unitarian church to which I belong, we have a celebration of new lives in which the congregation vows to help parents and children. Rev. Davidson Loehr wrote these lovely words for this ceremony, but they are fitting for any group where adults agree to care for the community's children.

> We give witness to our commitment to the sacredness of life and announce that we will be here as background support for these children and their parents, as the young ones grow in mind, body, and spirit. These children remind us of the fragility of our lives and our need for help from one another. These children come to life through us, but we do not own them. As the poet Kahlil Gibran has said, they are the sons and daughters of Life's longing for itself. We each have a part to play in

this drama of life . . . for we are all children of God, sons and daughters of Life's longing for itself, and the hope of the world. May we so live that our children will be able to acquire the best virtues and to leave behind our worst failings. May we pass on the light of courage and compassion; and may that light burn more brightly in these our children than it has in us.

These welcoming environments are good places where single mothers can go on to form an intentional community, a smaller group of people who commit to supporting each other on an ongoing basis. The type of support and activities can be negotiated by the group and may include taking care of each other's children, sharing cooperative meals a certain time each month, meeting regularly for check-in and support, or providing food or household help if a member is ill. If the members of an intentional community do not have relatives in the area, the group may choose to celebrate holidays and other special occasions together. Church is by no means the only place where this type of group can emerge. Single mothers at your workplace, at your children's day care or school, or at your community center may want to form an intentional community.

Richard Louv, a senior editor at Connect for Kids, a Web site sponsored by the Benton Foundation (www.connectforkids. org), warns that "isolation among parents helps create isolation among kids."

Louv told of one innovative single mom in San Diego who started a bartering network in her child's preschool. She was a hairdresser and offered to do another single mother's hair in exchange for birthday cakes, which was that single mom's specialty. The idea caught on and the school has hosted group sessions to link up more parents to determine what services could be traded.

Jody Seidler is another single mother who created an intentional community at her son's school because she needed a network. She enlisted the help of other single parents and through sign-up sheets at PTA meetings, flyers, and word of mouth, let people know that a group for single parents was being formed at the school. Forty people attended the first meeting. In less than three years, she had also organized groups for single parents at her work and synagogue, published articles on single parenting, and created a Web site for single parents called Making Lemonade (www.makinglemonade.com).

Louv also reported on some programs that link single-parent families who want to share housing. "By sharing the cost of a home, single parents can decrease the cost of housing, add to the comfort and size of the house, and get some baby-sitting relief, as well as added physical security and emotional support," he wrote. According to Louv, Innovative Housing in San Francisco, Lutheran Social Service's Share a Home in Minneapolis, and Nova Roommate Finders in San Diego are examples of what he calls the *Kate and Allie* model—the television show of several years ago in which two single mothers and their children form a household.

Connecting with other people to create community requires curiosity, courage, and confidence. But the rewards are worth the risks. If the idea of starting a network of single mothers seems totally out of character for you, start small. Find one other single mother with whom you can relate and ask her out for coffee. Keep your expectations reasonable and go slowly. Listen attentively to what she has to say and express yourself clearly, taking care not to get too intimate too soon. Build on your common experiences and concerns and, when and if the time seems right, bring up the idea of getting together occasionally with other single mothers.

Keep the definition of friend from *New Life, New Friends* in mind when you embark on any new relationship. Strive to establish "a mutual bond of respect, trust, and vulnerability that encourages healthy growth and acceptance." A community that has mutual respect as its cornerstone is a wonderful place to raise your children.

Take a Minute

Building Community

Community is built one step at a time, one friendship at a time.

Take a minute and think of a single mother you don't know well whom you would like to know better. Ask her to go out or come over for coffee. Practice friendship.

DISCOVERING A VIRTUAL COMMUNITY

"Don't struggle alone. Maximize your potential as a single parent by joining our extended family today," Andrea Engber urges the women who visit the National Organization of Single Mothers (NOSM) Web site (www.singlemothers.org). Engber, a syndicated columnist and coauthor of the book *The Complete Single Mother*, founded the nonprofit organization in 1991 for women she calls MOMs (Mothers Outside of Marriage).

NOSM is just one example of the great variety of Web sites available to single mothers. A virtual community cannot, nor should it, take the place of flesh-and-blood people and live person-to-person interaction, but the Internet can be a rich supplementary resource for single mothers who have access to a computer and modem. There are hundreds of articles written by experts on everything from how to collect child support to how to travel with young children, and resources where parents can get help and more information when they need it. Some sites, such as the excellent Connect for Kids, will e-mail newsletters that summarize issues and articles that will be discussed on its Web page each week. Winnowing out the best and most informative sites can be a little tricky at first, but I've included some at the back of this book that single moms might find helpful. These are good places to start, as many of them also provide links to other Web sites that might be of interest.

Perhaps best of all, with the click of a mouse, single mothers can be instantly connected to online support groups where they can get advice, compassion, and humor from other single mothers. As mothers dialogue with each other, connections are formed, and a community of cyber friends is established.

Take a Minute

Visiting a Virtual Community

A .06-second search at Google.com recently brought up almost 150,000 items when I entered the words "Single Mothers." While these are more choices than anyone, especially a busy single mother, wants to weed through, it is indicative of the vast amount of information available to single mothers on the Internet.

Take a minute and visit one of the Web sites listed at the back of this book. If you don't have Internet access, take the Web address with you the next time you visit your local library, where they should have a computer available for you to use. Look at the menu of options and see if something sparks your interest. Chat with another single mom if you want.

How did you enjoy your visit to this virtual community?

THREE

Of Mentors and Men

◫　◫　◫

> In the eyes of these children, what mattered was that they had
> a caring adult in their lives, someone to confide in, relax with,
> and look up to. But as a result, they were doing better in
> school and at home and avoiding violence and substance
> abuse—this at a pivotal time in their lives when even small
> changes in behavior, or choices made, can change the course of
> their future.
>
> —From Big Brothers Big Sisters of America Web site
> (www.bbbsa.org/March 2000)

THE IMPORTANCE OF MENTORS

It was Homer who first described the concept of mentoring
when he wrote the *Odyssey* and told how King Odysseus
asked his trusted friend Mentor to guide, protect, educate, and
nurture his son while the king went off to fight the Trojan War.

I wish I had known more about structured mentoring years
ago when a friend asked if I could be a "big friend" to his
teenage daughter who was having a hard time adjusting to her
parents' divorce. I would have been more regular and consistent in my visits with her, better at listening and doing check-
ins, clearer about goals—mine and hers. As it was, we bumped
along and did become friends, but she guided me as much as I

guided her. It wasn't until I took part in a planned mentoring program that I realized how much more I could have done.

Natural mentoring occurs through friendship, teaching, coaching, and counseling. Planned mentoring is more structured and involves programs that select and match participants through a more formal process. Mentors in structured mentoring programs can come from the corporate or professional world, religious communities, and neighborhoods to be connected with youth.

In the first nationwide impact study of a mentoring organization (Big Brothers Big Sisters of America), researchers from Public/Private Ventures found that young people who met regularly with mentors were:

- 46 percent less likely to begin using illegal drugs
- 27 percent less likely to begin using alcohol
- 53 percent less likely to skip school
- more confident of their performance in schoolwork
- less likely to hit someone
- able to get along better with their families

Most of the 959 boys and girls in the study were between the ages of ten and fourteen. More than 60 percent were boys; more than half were minorities. Most came from low-income households. Many lived in families with histories of substance abuse or domestic violence.

These statistics, which are detailed on the Big Brothers Big Sisters of America Web site, are significant for single mothers because they underscore what study after study reveals: children who have just one caring person outside the family who is actively involved in their lives have an even better chance of success. A mentor is *not* a foster parent or a "cool peer" or a therapist. Most important, a mentor is *not* a substitute for you. A mentor is a responsive adult who provides a young person with support, counsel, friendship, reinforcement, and positive role modeling. Mentors are good and respectful listeners who want to help young people recognize their potential. A successful mentorship builds on the values and strengths you've worked so hard to instill in your child.

In her book *Single Mothers by Choice*, Jane Mattes says that it is not healthy for a child to be raised in emotional isolation with a mother as the only source of nurturing, nor is it healthy for a mother to have her child be her sole source of emotional gratification. According to her, "One of the greatest gifts you can give your child is to let other caring people love him or her."

I first realized how crucial "listening presences" can be in young people's lives ten years ago when I interviewed a woman who worked with the Passamoquoddy Indian tribe in Pleasant Point, Maine. She told how eight "native brothers," as they called themselves, opened up the gym three nights a week and made themselves available to the young people on the reservation to play sports or just talk. An average of forty-five kids showed up each night. Just three years before this program began, the tribe spent $13,300 on windows that bored and angry children had vandalized. After the program was in place, they spent less than $100 on broken glass. About thirty tribal members also made a commitment to serve as positive role models by remaining drug- and alcohol-free and to teach the tribal language, drumming, singing, planting, as well as community values.

Consider mentorship for your children. Think about organizations in your community that might have mentoring opportunities that match your children's interests. Places such as Big Brothers Big Sisters (215-567-7000) have rigorous standards for mentor volunteers and require references and training to make sure the match will be a safe and appropriate one for the child. The National Mentoring Partnership (703-224-2200) can also direct you to local partnerships in your area.

If you and your children cannot locate a mentorship program, think about asking a friend to be a mentor to your child.

While some of the friends or teachers or coaches at school may already be informal mentors to your children, an acknowledged mentorship involves more of a regular commitment where the child and mentor get together at prearranged times. They might work on homework or just take a walk and talk; or they might role-play a job interview if your child is getting ready to enter the work world. They could go to a concert or movie or just hang out.

> My nephew is an adult now, but he spent a lot of time at my house when he was growing up. Not long ago we went for a walk together and, out of the blue, he said, "You know, when I was a teenager, a counselor at school asked me who made me feel safe, like I was a person worth listening to. I told him it was you." I just hugged him and started crying. I had no idea I made a difference in his life.

You're never too old to have a mentor—or, for that matter, you're never too old to be a mentor either. My friend Connie is in her eighties, and she continues to model behaviors I want to embrace. When her daughter came out to her, for example, she immediately went into "Connie drive" and found the nearest Parents and Friends of Lesbians and Gays group so she could learn how to be totally supportive of her daughter and her daughter's partner. Another friend of mine recently told me an experience she had with "trickle-down" role modeling.

> We had four generations of women in Washington at the Million Mom March, all marching together against gun violence. My ex-husband's eighty-nine-year-old mother walked with me, my daughter, daughter-in-law, and my four granddaughters. When I worried that it might be a long day, the great-grandmother of this clan just laughed and said, "You'll just have to try to keep up with me. . . ."

I've also watched my ex-sister-in-law carefully over the years to see how to be a better parent. She raised her five children on her own, with little money and with a sense of humor I still marvel at. Her kids are in their thirties now, and they adore her as much as her grandchildren do.

These relationships are all fertile ground on which to build a mentorship. Older friends or relatives often model behavior that is admirable. Asking them "Can you teach me that?" is the first step toward mentorship.

Saint Brigid told a cleric to "Go off and don't eat until you get a soul friend, because anyone without a soul friend is like a body without a head." Think about mentorship for both your children and yourself. It's a good way to keep your head.

TAKE A MINUTE

Finding a Mentor for Your Children

A caring mentor can make a huge difference in your child's life and can help ease some of the burden you may feel parenting alone. *Take a minute* and consider the benefits that might be gained through mentorship.

Find out about mentoring programs by asking family and friends who volunteer; someone in your workplace who handles community affairs; someone in your religious community who works with children or handles community outreach; or members of service clubs, civic groups, or professional associations you belong to. Call some of these places and ask them if they have any information they can send you. Ask them if they also have literature for children so you will be better prepared to discuss mentorship with your child. Determine what sort of commitment your child and the mentor are expected to make and whether or not the arrangement would work with your various schedules.

Narrow these possibilities and also list your friends or relatives who might make good mentors for your child. Look at your list and see which program or person seems most appropriate. Get clear on what this mentorship would involve before you discuss it with your child. If you are asking a friend to be a mentor, make certain he or she is willing to make the commitment before you talk to your child. Be positive and emphasize that the mentor wants to be involved in your child's life.

Take Another Minute

Finding a Mentor for Yourself

It's not only our children who need mentors. Positive role models can make a difference in our lives too. Bright Beginnings is a one-to-one mentoring program at North Memorial Health Care in Robbinsdale, Minnesota, designed to help teenage mothers get their infants off to a healthy start in life. Most of these mothers choose to raise their babies as single parents, but they have little knowledge of basic child development or how to access community services. Trained mentors provide friendship, support, social interaction, and guidance to the moms and work with them on finding ways to return to school, obtain good health and child care, housing, and other services.

Adult single mothers who cannot find a mentorship program may want to ask an older friend, relative, or acquaintance whose parenting skills they admire to be their parenting coach. Some of the most successful mentor/mentee relationships bring together very different people. An older mother who has been there and done that can help you find new and creative solutions to the challenges you face.

Take a minute and think about role models for yourself. Asking the following questions might help you narrow your choices:

- What qualities or traits does this person have that you think you want in terms of parenting?
- Does this person contribute honestly to a conversation without pretending to have all the answers?
- Does this person listen attentively?
- Can you imagine being vulnerable with this person?
- Can this person keep a confidence?
- Does this person have time to be an advisor?

If you answered yes to most of these questions, work up the courage and simply ask the prospect if she would be willing to be a parenting coach. The more clearly you state what you are looking for, the more clearly a prospective mentor can assess her ability to provide what you want. Remember that a mentor is not *your* parent. It is not her job to feed, clothe, employ, or monetarily support you. It is a mentor's job to be truthful, to be supportive and accepting, and to be available to help you be the best parent you can be, the best person you can be.

THE IMPORTANCE OF MEN IN CHILDREN'S LIVES

This is not one of those women-need-men-like-fish-need-bicycles books. I think it's important for both boys and girls to have good male role models in their lives. About half the population is male, so it makes sense that we teach our sons and daughters how to get along with men, just like we should teach them how to get along with the rest of humanity—people of different races, religions, sexual preferences, economic classes, or ages.

Many children have regular and healthy contact with their fathers, and that's good. The more loving people in a child's life, the better. But a man doesn't have to be "Daddy" to be a positive presence in your children's lives. This isn't about men versus women; it's about balance of experience. My mother taught Jessica how to bait a hook to fish, and her uncle taught her about car repair. Each such lesson rounds her personality and prepares her to live confidently.

Sometimes men can supply practical information that we might not have at our fingertips.

When my son was five, he became obsessed with the idea of playing hockey. Dutiful mother that I was, I went to our local park and rec and signed him up for the Bantam league. The coach gave me the list of equipment, and I spent my whole paycheck on skates, helmet, shin guards, mask, and a cup. When I took him to his first lesson, I discovered I had dressed him all wrong, all "inside out." I didn't know the shin guards were supposed to go under his pants. At least I had the cup in the right place. He was so embarrassed, and I felt like a total failure. I remember watching him discreetly trying to wipe his tears away, but he couldn't because of that damn mask.

This single mom went on to coach her son's soccer and T-ball teams, but she also got a solid male and female peer support system in place to prevent any future embarrassments like the hockey blunder.

Take a Minute

Finding Male Role Models

Take a minute and think about the men you know—siblings, cousins, coworkers, friends. . . . What qualities and abilities do they have that could positively influence your children? Do they interact respectfully with women and children? Which, if any, of these men would make good role models for your sons or daughters? Why?

FOUR

Mothering Yourself

After awhile you learn that kisses aren't contracts, and presents aren't promises.

And you begin to accept your defeats with your head up and your eyes ahead, with the grace of an adult, and learn to build all of your roads on today because tomorrow's ground is too uncertain for plans, and futures have a way of falling down in midflight.

After awhile you learn that even sunshine burns if you ask too much.

So you plant your own garden and decorate your own soul, instead of waiting for someone to bring you flowers.

And you learn that you really can endure, that you really are strong, and you really do have worth.

And you learn, and you learn, and you learn. . . .

—Author unknown

CAN YOU SPELL *CODEPENDENT*?

I am a slow learner when it comes to abstract concepts like "decorating my own soul" or concrete beliefs such as "I am worthy" or "I am strong." It took me until 1988—the birth of a child, a divorce, a remarriage, and forty-one years of other life experiences—to finally "get" that I counted, that my needs, desires, and feelings were worthy of attention.

I had flashes of insight during marriage counseling and my subsequent divorce, but those sparks were quickly snuffed out by my habit of charting my course by other people's compasses. I limped along for years, content to live in the shadow of others, convinced that other people mattered more, deserved more, because they were more important than I was. I became the poster child for resentful people pleasers.

Motherhood made my slide down the slippery slope of self-effacement even easier, because now I had a legitimate reason for ignoring myself. I poured myself into the role of devoted mother, sometimes invading Jessica's life as if it were my own. If she was happy, I was happy. If she was anxious or sad, I looked to myself for the cause or the cure. It was much easier to concentrate on her life than to take a hard look at my own, to identify the complex and confusing feelings I had buried after my former marriage and divorce.

I operated on autopilot for years, doing what needed to be done, continuing to put my emotions on hold or masking them with humor. I was the great little coper. I remember being a little perplexed when people expressed sympathy or admiration over how difficult it must have been for me to leave a marriage when my baby was just three months old, how hard it must have been to be a single mother. "You just do what you have to do," I'd tell them.

And then, fifteen years into a happy remarriage, when my mind signaled it was safe, I had a meltdown. I overheard a husband demeaning his wife in the produce aisle of the grocery store. He used the same tone of voice my former husband had used to belittle me so many times during our six-year relationship. All the feelings I thought I had successfully stuffed for so many years, began to surface, and I slipped into a despair that frightened me. The cheese stood alone. I could no longer hide behind the needs or feelings of others. It was time to learn how to tend to my own garden. A therapist helped me understand how important it is to acknowledge feelings when they arise, how necessary it is to take care of yourself so you can get the most out of your relationships with others and with life itself. I got clearer about who I was and what I needed. I worked up the courage to look at the pain, grief, loneliness, anger, confusion, doubt, and other emotions I had buried or transformed into other things such as anxiety, fear, low self-esteem, and people pleasing. I also started to learn that I could judge my own behavior and emotions instead of looking to others to evaluate me or my worth. I discovered the truth in the saying "My barn has burned down. Now I can see the moon."

I write this knowing full well that my journey is not your journey. I avoided taking care of myself by taking care of others, and then I retreated from others when I felt depressed. Some of you might deal with your emotions head-on; others might seek refuge in isolation. My problems are not the same as your problems, and my solutions will differ from yours. I do not pretend to have all the answers; God knows it took me long enough to realize I had deep questions. But I can offer some strategies for taking care of yourself, some ideas from experts on how to identify depression and lessen stress, and some things you might want to try that may decrease the pressures and increase the joys of single motherhood.

In his beautiful little book *Let Your Life Speak,* Parker J. Palmer writes, "By surviving passages of doubt and depression on the vocational journey, I have become clear about at least one thing: self-care is never a selfish act—it is simply good stewardship of the only gift I have, the gift I was put on earth to offer to others. Anytime we can listen to [our] true self and give it the care it requires, we do so not only for ourselves but for the many others whose lives we touch."

Andrea Engber and Leah Klungness, authors of *The Complete Single Mother,* emphasize that a commitment to self doesn't mean that "your children are left to their own devices while you pursue Zen meditation in some distant location," or that you accept a job that requires you to work one hundred hours a week. A commitment to self means "that you also have the responsibility to develop your own unique talents and skills to their fullest and not use your children as an excuse for not moving ahead with your own life."

TAKE TIME TO MAKE TIME

For many busy single mothers, the idea of carving out time for themselves probably sounds like one more thing to add to their to-do list. I know that when I'm feeling overwhelmed and under pressure, the last thing I want to see is some perky little model on television telling me how bath salts or flavored coffee can "take me away." "Like I have time for a bath!" I want to scream at them before I realize that if I weren't watching television, maybe I *would* have time for a bath.

> It is difficult for a single mom to be everywhere all the time, every game and activity. I tried to have relationships, work full-time, and go to school, and my kids suffered. So I dropped the relationships and unique time for myself.

There are hundreds of articles on how to organize your life and closets, and I won't attempt to replicate them here. There are some common ideas and tips, however, that you may want to consider as you go about your busy life as a single mom. All the articles I've seen on time management advise you to prioritize. The objective is for you to consciously choose what you need and want to do each day so you are spending more of your time the way you want to spend it. Sometimes it may be worth it to stay up late to clean if the mess in your house is getting to you. At other times you may opt for messiness in order to go to your child's soccer game or get some sleep.

I went to a community college when I was a single mom. In the mornings, I would get the kids off to elementary school, then drive to my school. I would take three classes in a row and then drive very fast to get home because my kindergartner would be coming home. During this time, I worked evenings and weekends. I studied late at night after the kids went to bed. Even though school made my life more hectic, it felt good. I liked talking with other adults and learning new things. Going to school gave me a feeling of moving forward with my life, of accomplishing something.

Make written lists of your daily activities and label the most urgent things you have to do. Cross off things as you accomplish them. Try to schedule appointments, like dental check-ups or haircuts, back-to-back so you can consolidate your trips. Put a family engagement calendar on the wall or refrigerator to record play dates, meetings, athletic practices and games, and personal and school events. I've seen special "Mom" calendars that have spaces to keep track of individual schedules, or you might want to use different colored Magic Markers to record your and your children's appointments.

Consolidate whenever possible. Try to plan your meals ahead, and set aside one day a week for your main grocery shopping and other errands. Chart your course ahead of time. Return the library books and videos first, for example, then go to the dry cleaners, and end up with the grocery store so your frozen items won't turn into liquid cuisine all over your trunk or backseat while you're in the hardware store. Use the telephone to find a store that has a particular item in stock rather than traveling all over town to locate it. Check your calendar ahead of time, and buy all birthday and anniversary cards a few months in advance. Have a good stock of note, sympathy, congratulations, and thank-you cards on hand so you don't have to make a special trip to the store each time an occasion arises. Try to pay your bills at one time; then divide them into two piles so you'll know which ones should be mailed at mid-month and which should be mailed at the end of the month. Sort important mail and discard junk mail immediately. Have a file folder or in-basket for your bills to be paid and a separate one for letters to be answered, and have one place where you keep your receipts after your bills are paid, so they will be readily accessible when you do your taxes. (This place should be yours alone, high enough or locked to avoid crayons and smeared Cheerios on your important papers.) Setting up a filing system that works for you can save you lots of time in the long run.

Enlist your children to help you with household chores and meals. Teach them how to make their own breakfast, how to set the table, load and empty the dishwasher, and clean their rooms. Praise them for their competence. Even young children can be assigned household responsibilities that can increase as they grow older.

> The kids are responsible for folding and putting away their napkins after a meal (and we get all sorts of interesting shapes!), and my son now makes his bed each morning (you could bounce a small boy, though not a quarter, off the quilt), and each child is responsible for putting dirty clothes in their laundry basket, hanging up coats, and bringing their dirty dishes to the counter.

Try to schedule a special time each day or evening for just you and your children so your children know this is their time to have your undivided attention.

> I don't know if it's because I lived in a single mother household, but my mom was like a playmate to us. I remember having special times after school. Sometimes she'd turn on her old records and we'd dance. Sometimes she'd be waiting for us with water balloons and

buckets, and all the kids in the neighborhood would have a water fight. Everyone loved it. For her birthday that year, the neighbors gave her a decorated water bucket.

Turn off the television; don't answer the phone or allow for other distractions. You might choose to read, play a game, dance, or just talk.

Bedtimes were tender times; we sang rounds and read together and to one another. It's one thing I miss now that they are grown-up and no longer live with me (besides missing them altogether, which I do, of course).

You could even use your special time for daily family meditation and discussion. About fifteen years ago, I had the good fortune to be one of the writers of *Today's Gift*, a family meditation book (published by Hazelden). Each day has a quote and an accompanying little story or fable that addresses that day's topic in a way that encourages discussion among children and parents. It's a helpful way to get children talking about tough subjects such as anger, hope, friends, or sadness, and it can increase their awareness of the world around them.

My children and I shared a spiritual life as well. We'd attend our Quaker meeting and talk about the relationship between the spiritual and political in terms of organizing, demonstrating, and caring together. It's probably what kept us a tight unit.

Of course there will be days when your best intentions will have to be thrown out the window.

I remember coming home from a long day at school and picking up the kids at day care only to learn they both had head lice. I had a lot of homework to do, but I needed to go immediately to the drugstore to get the proper remedies and cleaning supplies and go home and wash the kids, the bedding, all the clothes, and clean the house. I was exhausted.

Try to be gentle with yourself and your children during such detours and to accept them as just that—temporary bends in the road, not an exploded highway you can never return to again.

Finally, remember to *schedule*—not wish or try or hope, but actually set aside—time for just yourself. You might want to use Julia Cameron's idea of making an "artist's date" with yourself. In her popular book *The Artist's Way: A Spiritual Path to Higher Creativity,* Cameron tells people to set aside a block of time every week reserved only for you. You might take a walk, visit a museum, take yourself out to dinner, or curl up with a good book. The main thing is this your time. Treat it as sacred. Write it on your family's engagement calendar in bold letters; then highlight it with a neon Magic Marker. You might just convince yourself you deserve it, and you are modeling something invaluable to your children: the importance of tenderness to self.

My children seemed to know when I needed time off. One time they even offered to baby-sit me so I could have an "official" evening opportunity to be a kid.

Take a Minute

Setting Your Own Priorities

Writing down your priorities is a way to make sure that your agenda is truly your agenda—not your children's agenda or your boss's agenda or your friends' agenda.

Take a minute and write out the answers to the following questions:

- What do I need to accomplish today?
- What do I want to do for others or with others today?
- How will I go about accomplishing what I need and want to get done?
- How will I allow room for flexibility?

This sort of tracking makes us aware of the fragility or strength of our commitments. We can see how we set out to do something and how we let ourselves get pulled aside.

As we observe the ebb and flow of our thoughts and actions, we realize how others are living with similar shifts and changes. Compassion grows. We learn to assess our decisions, to redirect and forgive ourselves and others for not being perfect.

CHANGE WHAT YOU CAN CHANGE

Taking care of ourselves means taking responsibility for the consequences of our own actions and reactions and understanding what we can and cannot control. In Alcoholics Anonymous (AA) parlance, this means accepting the things we cannot change, having the courage to change the things we can, and seeking the wisdom to know the difference. These are the components of the Serenity Prayer, which is often referred to in AA.

By taking personal responsibility, we move beyond blame and shame. We realize that we control our own thoughts and actions. We are bound to make mistakes, but we don't punish ourselves unmercifully for them; we learn from our mistakes and move on. We learn to quiet that incessant chatterbox inside our head that drones on and on with negative self-talk and replace it instead with a loving voice that convinces us we are strong and worthy. We understand that we have choices and that we can choose to take the path that contributes most to our personal growth and happiness.

The idea that our feelings result from the messages we give ourselves is at the heart of cognitive therapy. In *Feeling Good: The New Mood Therapy*—probably the best-known book on the subject—Dr. David Burns explains that our thoughts or perceptions (our "cognitions") often have more to do with how we feel than with what is actually happening in our lives. In other words, our attitudes can direct our feelings.

When I went through my dark time, I didn't realize how distorted my thinking was. *I* made sense to *me*. After hard work and professional guidance, I was able to understand what Burns talks about when he writes, "When you are depressed, you possess the remarkable ability to believe, and to get the people around you to believe, things which have no basis in reality." Instead of looking inward for the cause of my unhappiness, I convinced myself and others that it was the weather or my boss or some other external force that was the problem.

One of the first things my therapist did was have me read Burns's book, and, after some time, I felt like a curtain had been lifted. There wasn't a wizard behind it, only a mirror, only me pulling the levers, controlling the thoughts. I was both elated and terrified to realize how powerful my thoughts were and how negative or distorted thoughts—what recovering alcoholics might call "stinking thinking"—could paralyze me.

When you slip into distorted thinking, you have a tendency to see the world as black and white. You believe things always happen to you; you see only the negative in something or transform positive experiences into negative ones. Burns says that distorted thinkers are often convinced others are looking down on them and jump to negative conclusions. (If a friend doesn't call or if someone isn't paying close enough attention to you, that person *must* hate you.) Distorted thinkers think at the extremes. They might magnify their faults out of proportion while they play down any strengths they have. They may also confuse their emotions with facts. It's an "I feel therefore it is" approach to life. (If I'm angry with you, you *must* have done something contrary.) Burns says people in despair also have a "shouldy" approach to life, beating themselves up for what they think they should and shouldn't do, ultimately creating self-loathing, shame, and guilt because they feel they are constantly falling short of their expectations. Distorted thinkers also label themselves based on their failures ("I'm such a loser") and take responsibility for any negative happening. (If my child misbehaves, it means I'm a bad mother.)

Distorted thinkers don't blame only themselves. To feel better about themselves, they often blame others for their unhappiness. (The clerk at the store put me in a bad mood; my friend made me miss exercise class; my boss made me look stupid; the mechanic hates women; God is punishing me.) They avoid taking responsibility by holding others responsible. But they gradually feel worse; as their list of scapegoats gets longer, their trust level plummets, and their sadness intensifies.

Not all sadness is depression, of course, and no two people are sad in the same way. It's normal to feel downhearted sometimes, but we usually feel better within a few days. Depression, however, is an illness that can last for months or years if it is left untreated. The American Psychiatric Association, as cited by Dr. Isadore Rosenfeld, advises you to get help if you have experienced five or more of the following symptoms for two or more consecutive weeks:

- significant weight loss or gain
- insomnia or sleeping too much
- lack of energy and frequent fatigue
- feelings of worthlessness and inappropriate guilt
- restlessness and irritability
- difficulty thinking, making decisions, or concentrating
- thoughts of death or suicide or attempts at suicide

The first real bout of depression that I am aware of was when my daughter left home to go to college out of state. I was devastated. We had been inseparable up until then, and yet I knew this is what she needed. I also had recently ended a serious relationship and felt horribly alone. All of this was intensified by problems at work that caused everything to come to a head. Thank God I had a very good friend at work who recognized the symptoms and literally took me by the hand to the nurse's office. I went through both group and individual counseling and was on antidepressant medication for about two years.

This single mother was lucky that she had a concerned friend who intervened when she needed help, but don't wait for such intervention if you are experiencing symptoms of depression that won't go away. The National Mental Health

Association offers a confidential screening for depression at its Web site (www.depression-screening.org) that may help you determine if you should seek professional help. As with any other illness, you should see your doctor if you think you might be depressed. The Campaign on Clinical Depression, sponsored by the National Mental Health Association, also provides free information on depression, its treatment, and local screening sites (800-228-1114).

I still slip into distorted thinking at times, convincing myself that I am worthless or that something or someone else is causing me to feel the way I do, forgetting that I control my own thoughts and actions. My negative thoughts are a signal to me that I need to take a closer look at how I'm thinking. At such times, I'll talk to a good listening friend and catch myself in some distortion, or I'll use a journal exercise that I've found useful, or I'll reread Burns's book and do some of his suggested exercises. If the negative cloud won't lift, despite my best efforts, I will call my therapist for what I call a "booster shot"—a session or two to sort things out and get back on track, back to the middle, more balanced ground.

In *Life's Companion*, Christina Baldwin quotes an unknown author who wrote, "When you come to the edge of all that you know, you must believe one of two things: There will be earth to stand on, or you will be given wings to fly." One antidote for despair is trust. Our confusion and negativity will lift with time and tenderness. Time, tenderness, and trust. Say the words out loud. Make them your mantra of self-care.

Take a Minute

Dialogue with Self

I first learned the technique of dialoguing with myself years ago in one of the first writing classes I took. The instructor had us "talk back" to our internal censor—that little guy who sits on our shoulder hissing in our ear about how worthless we are and how lousy our writing is. First I let him talk (for some reason, my internal critics are always male), and then I responded. It felt freeing to take him on, to defend myself on the page.

I have run across variations on the internal dialogue theme many times since my initial experience in that writing class. Therapists use it, creativity coaches use it, self-help books use it, and other writers use it in their how-to books. Having a conversation with yourself on the page can be an effective way to interrupt the stream of negative and distorted thoughts that may run through your mind when you feel in conflict, despair, or overcome with self-doubt. When you tell yourself things such as "I am such a lousy mother," your softer, more rational self can recount the sweet time you had with your child the day before, the successful conversation you shared, the funny incident that made you both laugh hysterically.

Take a minute the next time you are feeling down or stuck, and have a conversation in your journal with yourself. You might want to give the two speakers names. My friend calls hers Blaming Betty and Really Rosie. A dialogue might go like this:

> **Critical Self:** "I never do anything right."
> **Softer Self:** "That's silly. You do lots of things right. Just today you remembered to send your mother a card, you met a deadline, and you helped an elderly woman find her car."

Critical Self: "I'm lazy, and my house is always a mess. All my friends are able to exercise, work, and keep their houses immaculate."

Softer Self: "You were up until 2:00 A.M. working and got up to do laundry at 8:00 before you left. Maybe you can find time for a nap or a walk later. I think your friends feel overwhelmed too. Don't you remember S. telling you how she threw all her clutter in her closet when the doorbell rang?"

Critical Self: "I never carry through with things. I planned to clean last night, then my son came over and we went out for dinner."

Softer Self: "That sounds like fun. You were just saying how sad you were that you haven't seen Jason lately. Sounds like a good choice to me. Would you rather have been cleaning?"

Critical Self: "No, you're right. It was a special night. I guess vacuuming can wait."

Well, you get the idea. When I dialogue with myself, my distorted thoughts are usually quieted by my more rational self. You might also try having a conversation in your journal with another person. Let your children "speak" to you on the page when you are feeling angry or confused about their behavior; let your friend who hurt you "explain" herself. I've even had a "conversation" with my dead grandmother, asking for her wise counsel and imagining her responses. Of course, it is really me who holds the answers, but these dialogues help me correct my perspective and gain a clearer understanding of others in the process. They help me realize that I know more than I think I do.

STRESS MANAGEMENT

All parenting—all living, for that matter—involves stress, and not all stress is bad. Stress performs an important function in our lives. If a small child runs into the street, for example, our body's stress alarm system jolts us into action. Our heart rate speeds up and adrenaline pumps through us, allowing us to react quickly. We swoop the child up, plant her on safe ground, and breathe deeply once the danger has passed.

Stress in crises can save us, and prolonged and excessive stress can lead to medical problems and depression, which we've already discussed. Most of the time, however, we're faced with the ordinary, garden-variety type of stress that comes and goes as we go about our busy lives. Stress has become an accepted condition of modern life for everyone, even our children. As David Elkind points out in *The Hurried Child* and in *All Grown Up and No Place to Go,* pediatricians are noticing a greater number of stress-related ailments (headaches, stomachaches, etc.) in today's children than in previous generations. Elkind says that psychological stress usually involves a conflict between self and society. When we satisfy a social demand at the expense of a personal need, or vice versa, we create new demands and new stress. If we devote too much time to work, for example, our obligations at home grow along with our stress.

> I think fatigue is a real problem for single mothers. I picked my youngest son up from day care one day after work, drove home, and drove almost in a hypnotic state, right into the garage door.

For single mothers who are usually on call twenty-four hours a day, stress can be a constant though unwelcome companion. Symptoms of stress such as tension headaches, fatigue, and irritability become so familiar, they often go unchecked. But these symptoms are related to that same instinctive response that causes us to rescue a child from danger. They are our body's way of telling us that we need to take notice, to pull back and slow down, if even for a moment.

We know from the volumes that have been written on stress management that we all need to get enough sleep, eat nutritiously, and exercise. Yet naps, vegetables, and yoga are the last things on your mind when your child has just shaved the cat or your boss has asked you to work late for the third time that week. A. Jayne Major, founder of the Parent Connection in Los Angeles, suggests that single parents take a time-out when a stressful situation arises. Counting to ten, breathing evenly and deeply, changing the subject, and taking a walk or a drive are some ways to take a time-out. The goal, she says, is to give yourself enough time to shift from the tension to being relaxed so you can deal with the situation calmly and wisely. When we calm down a bit, we often realize that it is our perception of the event—not the event itself—that is causing us to feel stressed. It's amazing how one objective moment can provide hours, even days of clarity.

Another stress-busting technique is contained in the two-letter word "no." It's perfectly okay to decline an invitation once in a while, to tell the PTA president you aren't able to chair this year's fun fair but you would be happy to bake some bars or help in some other way. It's all right to ask friends and relatives not to call during dinner or your children's story time, and it's all right to tell people you will call them back if they do call at an inconvenient time. It's fine to ask people not to stop by without notice. It's even permissible to say no to your children when they beg for an unnecessary toy or pair of designer jeans. If they really want something that you do not choose or cannot afford to buy them, you can suggest they spend their own money on it. And when you're dog tired and overwhelmed, it's okay to say no to household chores once in a while and yes to a long soak in the tub or a few more hours of sleep.

The greatest challenge for single mothers is finding time for you. You are with your kids all the time with no break. My kids went some weekends with their dad, but he was inconsistent and often didn't show up for required visits, so it was impossible to plan anything for my time off. This is especially difficult for me—a very introverted person who needs a lot of time alone to recharge my energy. It was hardest when my kids were little and I was struggling on welfare. It's easier now that they're older. They can sleep over at their friends' houses once in a while, and they go to summer camp. I still have trouble, though, finding the balance between personal life and parenting responsibilities.

It may be tempting to use drugs or alcohol to numb unpleasant feelings or reduce stress, but such measures only mask reality for a short time. If you develop a habit of turning to alcohol or drugs to escape your problems, you could make things worse.

I remember everything that reminds me of my mom's drinking problem. The big plastic cups that she used to drink her vodka and orange juice in, the way she sat when I knew she had been drinking, the way she acted, just everything. I never knew my dad, so it was just Mom and my sister and me. I didn't bring my friends home at all because of my mom's alcohol abuse. I remember one time when I was about ten and my mom was fighting with one of her boyfriends. She pulled the phone out of the wall, threw it, and it hit me right in the head. I had a huge bump, but my mom couldn't even remember doing it, so I just said I fell off the swing set at school. My grandma worried about us constantly, and I finally moved in with her just to get away from my mom. Everyone in our family was affected by my mother's drinking.

No mother wants to leave a legacy of memories like these for her children. Please get help if your drinking or drug use has reached a point where it interferes with your ability to function in any area of your life. Call the Center for Substance Abuse Treatment hotline (800-662-HELP) if you can answer yes to some of these questions and think you might have a problem with drug or alcohol abuse:

- Do you use more alcohol or other drugs than you did in the past?
- Do you use more alcohol or other drugs than you intended or for longer times than you intended?
- Do you spend a lot of time thinking about using alcohol or other drugs—and making plans to get them?
- When you stop using alcohol or other drugs, do you get sick or anxious?
- Have you had to change your activities (work, social, family) so that you could use alcohol or other drugs?
- Have you tried to quit or control your use of alcohol or other drugs—and failed?
- Do you continue to use alcohol or other drugs—even when bad things happen to you (accidents, legal issues, family problems, work problems)?
- Have any of your friends or family members expressed concern about your alcohol or drug use?

When you seek help for drug or alcohol dependency, you send your children the message that you care enough about yourself and them to change your life. How you deal with your own alcohol and drug use or abuse can greatly influence the way your children will think about drugs and alcohol. Recovery can provide unexpected opportunities to talk with your children about chemical dependency and other issues that affect their own lives. The lessons you've learned can help them make more informed—and healthier—choices for themselves.

If you or your former spouse are in recovery from drug or

alcohol abuse, it might be wise to involve your children in an Alateen or Alatot support group so they can have a safe place in which to discuss their thoughts and feelings with children their own age. You can find meetings in your area by calling 888-4AL-ANON. Letting others support and comfort your children is a sign of strength, as a parent, not a parenting deficit.

Stress is often compared to the tension in a violin string. If there is too much tension, the string snaps. If the string is too loose, the sound is listless and hollow. Again, it comes back to balance. A little stress can energize us and keep us sharp; too much stress can break us. When we tune in to our bodies and our minds, slow down a little, and take care of ourselves, we strike a balance. We realize that we can compose the music of our own lives.

Take a Minute

Mothering Yourself

It's a good idea to pause every now and again to take your emotional, physical, mental, and spiritual pulse in order to track how well you are taking care of yourself. *Take a minute* to reflect upon the previous week and ask yourself:

- Am I honoring my body? Have I listened to its aches, tensions, and feelings? Did I take time to rest when I was tired? Did I get some exercise? Did I eat balanced and healthy meals?
- Am I honoring my mind? Have I taken the time to read a good book, take an interesting class, or learn something new? Was I able to exchange ideas and talk about opinions with a friend?
- Am I honoring my emotions? Was I able to express my feelings in my journal or to another person? Have I spent quality time with someone this week? Did I take time to play and laugh? Did I give myself time to cry when I needed to?
- Am I honoring my spirit and soul? Have I spent time in prayer, meditation, or solitary thought? Have I taken the time to be quiet with myself and with nature? Have I read something inspirational or listened to beautiful music?

Keep this list handy and refer to it often. Use it as a reminder to keep your life in balance.

LEARNING TO FORGIVE

The writer Anne Lamott recalled hearing that forgiveness is giving up all hope of having had a different past. That definition is particularly useful for divorced or separated single mothers. Although there is such a thing as an amicable breakup, many partnerships end in bitterness, grief, or anger. Whether you chose to leave your spouse or your spouse left you, the residue of your relationship remains long after you've parted company. As I discovered, the ghost of your former relationship and partner can come back to haunt you and your children years after you've severed all physical connection. Things get even more challenging for those who deal with visitation, support, and other parenting issues, because the person you've divorced is still present in your life.

In an on-line article, author Vicki Lansky wrote that "divorce, unlike marriage, is forever when there are kids." It is hard for parents who may no longer even like each other to remember that it is they, and not their children, who chose to get divorced.

> My parents never put us in the middle or talked down about each other. When we were younger, my mother encouraged our relationship with my father and his family. She never used us kids as weapons or kept us from our dad. It wasn't until I was much older and started seeing things on my own that my mother told me some of what went on with my dad. He was an alcoholic, and she could have easily turned us against him, but she wanted us to know our father and his family. I am very grateful for this, especially now that I am an adult and he has been sober for fifteen years. I know my grandmother has said many times that she is so thankful my mother allowed them to be involved in our lives. Now my kids can

know him as their grandpa. They also have a special relationship with their great-grandparents.

A child has a right to love both parents, and it is important that you do not put your children in the middle of a battleground between you and your former partner. It is also important that your children know that they had nothing to do with the breakup, and it is not their fault if the absentee parent chooses not to be involved in their lives.

> My daughter's father moved around frequently and didn't really have a consistent, dependable, or mature relationship with her. That was especially hard when she was young. He would oftentimes call her up and tell her he was coming to visit, and then he just wouldn't show up. She would be all packed and excited, and he would disappoint her time and again. Although I tried to never say anything bad about him, I finally had to put a stop to that. As she grew up, I let her make the decisions about how much time she wanted to spend with her dad. Unfortunately for him, by the time he was ready to have a real relationship with her, she was in college and had already made all of her decisions about her future without him. It was too little, too late. At present, and by her choice, she has no contact with him at all.

Of course, children don't *have* to love their fathers. Many single mothers fled from relationships in which they and their children were abused and mistreated. The Center for the Prevention of Sexual and Domestic Violence (www.cpsdv.org) reports that wife beating results in more injuries requiring medical treatment than rape, auto accidents, and muggings combined. They say to call your local police or the Domestic Violence hotline (800-799-7233) if you need help in a crisis. The most important job a mother has under such circumstances is to protect herself and her children.

I lived with an abusive alcoholic for nine years. When our daughter was seven and our son was three, things got so bad that I had to go to a woman's crisis center. I was there for a month, then moved to an apartment and got a divorce. It was very difficult dealing with an angry, vindictive person who was unwilling to compromise. I had to have help from lawyers, social workers, family court, mediation, and counselors. I've been a single parent for almost ten years now, but no matter how hard it gets, it's better than being in that painful, unhappy marriage.

Get help if you or your children are victims of domestic violence. You have a right to be safe, and you have a duty to protect your children. Let the experts handle any negotiations or communication with the abuser. They can also help you explain to your children what has happened and why you needed to take the action you did.

Try not to bad-mouth your former spouse to your children, no matter how justifiable your rage may be. As these friends discovered, you don't have to censor your feelings, just your discussion of your feelings.

My friend and I have agreed to be mutual "dumping grounds" for each other. If we are feeling intensely frustrated, confused, hurt, or angry with our former spouses or even with our children, we vent our emotions with each other first. "Tell me everything you'd like to tell him," my friend will say. Sometimes this feels like I'm taking my thumb out of a dam. My rage and pain just gush out. I don't have to make sense or worry whether or not I'm being nice or fair or rational. We don't judge or correct each other. We just listen, and usually the "dumpee" gets clearer about the issue, her reaction to it, and the course of action she should take. By using each other this way, we avoid saying something to our kids that we'll regret later.

Your child is your child, not your therapist, support group, or close friend in the "I can tell you anything in the world" sort of friendship way. Answer your children's questions as honestly as seems appropriate. Let them express their feelings about the other parent or the divorce and try your best to listen empathetically, without editorializing ("I know just what you mean. He used to treat me that way too. I remember the time . . .").

Respect and maintain your parent/child boundaries and try not to use your children as sounding boards. Don't complain to them about missed support payments or visitation. Contact your lawyer if your ex is not abiding by the terms of the divorce, or call your state's Human Services Department (office of child-support enforcement) if your former spouse is in arrears on child support.

Do not use your children as spies or messengers either, no matter how tempted you may be. If your former spouse needs to know something, communicate with him or her directly or through your lawyer or mediator if the lines of communication have broken down.

The courts dealt out all of our visitation. I gave my lawyer a visitation and holiday schedule. The judge gave my ex Mondays, Wednesdays, and every other weekend. I don't really have much communication with him with regard to those things taken care of in court. That's what my lawyer is for. I do keep my ex informed of doctor visits and general ideas related to our daughter's day-to-day stuff.

If it is possible, try to maintain a good working relationship with your former spouse if he or she is actively involved in your children's lives. If you can work together to set consistent household rules and discipline practices, the transition from one house to the other during scheduled visitation will be smoother because children know what to expect.

My mother was very good about not saying negative things about my father. They got along well and never openly fought in front of us. She backed him up when we were mad at him. He had the same rules for his household as my mom did, and their discipline was pretty much the same.

Working together with your former spouse to present a united parenting front to your children can prevent problems in the future.

As the kids got older, there was a lot of "Mom says no, so I'll just ask Dad and he'll say yes because he wants me to be happy and he likes to get my mom pissed off." That situation was so maddening to me. Raising kids is hard enough, even under the most perfect of circumstances. When someone is purposefully undercutting your decisions and making it seem like you're always the bad guy, it makes it even more challenging.

If it's feasible, keep your former spouse informed about school and extracurricular activities, parent-teacher conferences, and other matters of mutual concern and interest. Be sure to form a good relationship with your children's teachers so they can let you know if there are any problems with your child's behavior or academic performance. Let teachers know if you are going through a divorce or difficult time, and invite them to contact you directly if your child appears to be having problems in school.

As a teacher, I have been involved with many successful single parents and their children. The most successful situations seem to be ones where the parents are actively involved with their children and share appropriate information with the school. I got a note from one of my students' mothers advising that he was going to have a change in his home situation and that she could be contacted at work if I noticed any change in his behavior. This allowed me to provide extra support for a very nice little boy during a difficult time. I contacted his mom and told her of our school guidance counselor's group for children of divorced parents, and she readily agreed that her son might benefit from this group. As the year went on, I was asked to provide copies of his progress report and report card to his dad. When conference time came, both of his parents came together and agreed to share the responsibility for the suggestions I made about his schoolwork.

Regardless of their personal feelings toward each other, these parents worked together to provide a supportive, loving environment for their son.

In *Life's Companion,* Christina Baldwin wrote that "Forgiveness is the act of admitting we are like other people. The only choice we have is to reconcile ourselves to our own flaws and the flaws of other people, or withdraw from the community. . . . You have to decide: Are you going on a journey to see what love can accomplish, or are you going on a journey to see what revenge, blame, and hostility can accomplish?"

The past has passed. We cannot change what was, but we can kiss our wounds, dry our tears, and walk hand in hand with our children toward a bright tomorrow.

EMBRACING IMPERFECTION

In her meditation book *Meditations for Women Who Do Too Much,* Anne Wilson Schaef calls perfectionism "self-abuse of the highest order." When we expect perfection, we operate in a world of illusion. We judge ourselves by impossible standards and berate ourselves when we fail to meet our unreachable goals. We drive ourselves crazy rushing about trying to be the perfect mother, perfect employee, perfect friend, and perfect woman. This means, of course, that our children must be the perfect children too, because we cannot be perfect mothers if our children are imperfect.

Perfectionism ultimately leads to disappointment because perfectionists are never satisfied. They live in an "if only," "less than," and "should be" world where success is always around the corner, always out of reach.

I never viewed myself as a perfectionist because I pictured a perfectionist as a person with an immaculate house and a sixty-hour-per-week job. Since it takes very little arm twisting for a friend to lure me away from housecleaning or my office, I did not fit my definition of a perfectionist. I have come to realize, however, that I *was* a perfectionist when it came to relationships. I set impossible standards for myself, for my friends, and for my little family; then I'd get distressed when all of us fell short of my lofty expectations. My pursuit of interpersonal excellence was a joyless journey, and I am much happier now that I see myself and my friends as "perfectly adequate."

In his book *Feeling Good,* Dr. Burns suggests that perfectionists make a list of the advantages and disadvantages of being perfectionistic. He predicts that when they see how the disadvantages (it makes me nervous; I'm afraid of making a mistake; I get self-critical; I can't relax; it make me impatient with others; it keeps me from taking risks; it isn't any fun; it makes me inefficient; it helps me procrastinate) can outweigh the advantages (it makes me work hard), they will relax a bit and not try so desperately to be perfect.

Being (or trying to be) the perfect mother, friend, and relative often made me feel generous, sensitive, and caring. However, I also felt resentful and unappreciated at times, personally depleted because I rushed to care for everyone else instead of pausing to care for myself, guilty if I forgot a birthday or important anniversary, and disappointed when others didn't return my nurturing gestures. I know now (because I've surveyed my loved ones about this) that my devotion often made them uncomfortable because it was so out of balance in terms of what they were willing or able to give back. I discovered that it was more important to simply be present with my friends and less important to remember that their aunt Martha twice removed was having eye surgery. I also learned that deep friendship happens when people are willing to be mutually vulnerable with each other. My friends didn't want or expect me to be Mother Teresa. They were *perfectly* willing to accept me as *me,* in all my splendid imperfection.

Progress, not perfection. Progress, not perfection. Say it with feeling; capture the rhythm of the phrase. It chugs along like the little engine in the story we read to our children. The goal for single mothers—the goal for everyone, for that matter—is to move forward, one day, one experience, and, yes, even one mistake at a time. You will not be a perfect mother. Your children will not be perfect children. But you can be a loving mother, a good friend, and a fine human being, capable of learning from, even laughing at, your foibles.

I have a *Shoe* cartoon by Jeff MacNelly taped to my desk in which Professor Cosmo Fishhawk asks the Padre bird if he's heard any good prayers lately. The Padre responds with the Serenity Prayer ("God, grant me the serenity to accept the things I cannot change, the courage to change the things I can, and the wisdom to know the difference"). The Padre explains how the prayer comes in handy a lot, but that he actually prefers the short version: "Lighten up."

If perfectionism is the disease, laughter just might be the cure. Laughter truly is good medicine. A smile, a twinkle in the eye, or a good-natured chuckle can keep us on track and remind us to lighten up. Laughing is another way of taking care of ourselves. Laughter is, Schaef says, "like the human body wagging its tail." I love that image of pure delight, of wiggling things into perspective.

When I open myself to the humor around me, my day seems less stressful. I feel lighter and more relaxed, better able to meet the demands and challenges ahead. When I open myself to humor, I find it in the oddest places. For instance, I laughed out loud not long ago when I read the obituary of a stranger named Bob Matzke. He had a little message embedded in his death notice entitled "The Wisdom of Bob Matzke." It read: "You're born, you die . . . and you become fertilizer for the plants of the earth, the natural cycle of life. The grass grows and is eaten by a horse . . . and it too passes through a certain natural cycle. So next time you see a pile of horse manure, don't kick it, it could be me. Thanks everyone; it was a great journey." I don't know who Bob Matzke was, but I like this stranger who made me laugh.

Ralph Waldo Emerson said that success is the ability:

To laugh often and love much; to win the respect of intelligent persons and the affection of children . . . to appreciate beauty; to find the best in others; to give of one's self; to leave the world a bit better, whether by a healthy child, a garden patch, or a redeemed social condition; to have played and laughed with enthusiasm and sung with exultation; to know even one life has breathed easier because you have lived. This is to have succeeded.

His definition includes no mention of fame or fortune. It does not say you have to strive to be perfect or sacrifice your health or well-being to achieve some impossible goal. Emerson says laugh, play, sing, love, and stop to notice the beauty around you, and you will succeed. Go ahead, "plant your own garden and decorate your own soul. . . . And you learn, and you learn, and you learn. . . ."

Take a Minute

A Blessing a Day

I was in a local malt shop one afternoon when a young mother and her two children in the next booth caught my attention. After they got settled and placed their order, the mom turned to her son and daughter and asked, "What did you learn today and what made you laugh?" The question seemed comfortable and routine, a daily practice for this family. With this simple ritual, this mother was giving her children permission to slow down and notice the wonder around them each day. She was leading them down Emerson's path of success by encouraging them to laugh and learn.

Remember that old song that had the line in it "Just count your blessings instead of sheep, and you'll go to sleep counting your blessings"? Noticing the goodness that surrounds me is one of the best things I do to take care of myself. When I was in a particular slump, my friend Christina suggested that I start a "Blessing a Day Journal." She said that before I went to sleep each night, I should write down the gifts I had been given that day. I got a special little book and wrote "My Blessings" on the cover. Each night I'd record things such as "Beautiful sunset. The quality of light through the morning mist. The laughter of children in the park. The call from my mom saying she's proud of me."

After about a week, I was looking at the world differently. Instead of feeling irritated when it rained, I noticed how the rain glistened and danced on the window. Spider webs intrigued me; people delighted me. No matter how angry, sad, or frustrated I got during the day, my spirits would lift at day's end when I took the time to write down the gifts I had been given. And I'd often awaken greedy to see what the new day held.

Take a minute and review your day, concentrating on the

gifts you were given. Use your five senses (hearing, seeing, feeling, smelling, and tasting) to help you remember the good things you experienced. Did you hear people interacting in a special way? What did you notice in nature? Did your child hug you or show you affection? Did you eat a delicious meal with a friend? Did you laugh? Did you learn?

You may want to get a special little notebook for your blessings. You might want to start a "family blessings" journal in which you and your children can record your individual gifts and see how all your blessings multiply when they are recorded together, or your children may want to start a journal of their own.

Ann Ruth Schabacker wrote that "Each day comes bearing its gifts. Untie the ribbons." Stop and notice what the day and the world are giving you. Remember to say thank you to others and to yourself, and try to laugh at least once every day.

FIVE

Raising Resilient Children

■ ■ ■

> At every step the child should be allowed to meet the real experiences of life; the thorns should never be picked from the roses.
>
> —From *The Century of the Child* by Ellen Key (1909)

EXPERIENCE MAKES US STRONG

There are entire days now, thirty years after my divorce, when I can actually muster up appreciation for my former husband and our short-lived courtship and marriage. Things like driving thirty-five miles to my doctor's office alone on a Minnesota March morning, with contractions only minutes apart, because he didn't want to leave work, toughened me up. And I probably wouldn't have gone to college if he hadn't repeatedly told me how stupid I was. His taunting fueled both my desire for higher learning and my need to prove him wrong. While I wouldn't wish these experiences on anyone, I'm a stronger person because I had them. And he did help create Jessica, the most precious of gifts that continues to keep on giving. When I focus on the lessons learned and the gift given, I'm able to practice what recovering alcoholics call an attitude of gratitude. For me, having an attitude of gratitude isn't the same as believing that it's necessary to suffer in order to grow;

rather, it's developing a sense of appreciation for the insights gained from *all* of life's lessons—good and bad alike.

It is natural to want to shield our children from the difficult lessons of life, to pluck the thorns from the roses so they won't get pricked by painful experience. But no matter how vigorously we try, we can't protect them from every life trial any more than my mother could protect me.

> I naïvely thought my son would have no ill effects from the divorce because he never really knew his biological father, and his stepfather adopted him when he was just a toddler. Imagine my surprise (and guilt) when he ended up in therapy as an adult because he had abandonment issues that stemmed from his natural father leaving him.

No matter how certain we are about becoming or being a single mother, we will have moments of doubt about the ways this decision might affect our children. We hear statistics about drug and alcohol use among teens, about the rising rates of attention deficit disorder and depression among children and worry about our own kids. When researchers tell us these problems are more prevalent in single-parent homes, we usually don't stop to question the study; we immediately question our ability to parent, and our worry turns to guilt. It doesn't matter if some of the adverse effects noted by researchers were there before a divorce or stemmed from other factors, or that some of the study results are skewed because they haven't adequately controlled for variables such as economic loss or biased reporting. It's hard to squash that seed of doubt once it's been planted.

It is not my purpose to debate the validity of various reports or statistics. I think it's enough to realize that all children are faced with challenges, pressures, and opportunities on a daily basis. Children of single mothers probably do face more challenges, just as single mothers face more challenges than mothers with partners. Lack of time and money were two common complaints among the women and children I heard from. It is not our job to protect our children from life. It *is* our job to ready them to meet life's challenges with grace and confidence so they can discover how they might turn the challenges into opportunities.

Sometimes a bit of a struggle makes us more complete. A friend sent me a lovely little story that illustrates this truth nicely: Once upon a time, a man found the cocoon of a butterfly. He sat and watched the small opening of the cocoon as the butterfly struggled to force its body through the little hole. It tried and tried to emerge but seemed to be making no progress, so the man decided to help it out by taking a pair of scissors and carefully snipping off the remaining bit of the cocoon. The butterfly crawled out easily, but it had a swollen body and small, shriveled wings that never got bigger. It was never able to fly.

What the man, with all his good intentions, did not understand was that the restricting cocoon and struggle to emerge were nature's way of forcing fluid from the body of the butterfly into its wings so it would be ready for flight once it achieved its freedom from the cocoon. The butterfly was crippled without this struggle.

The little story was accompanied by an anonymous poem, part of which reads:

> I asked for strength, and God gave me difficulties to make me strong.
> I asked for wisdom, and God gave me problems to solve.
> I asked for prosperity, and God gave me brain and brawn to work.
> I asked for courage, and God gave me danger to overcome.
> I asked for love, and God gave me troubled people to help.

I asked for favors, and God gave me opportunities.
I received nothing I wanted.
I received everything I needed.

We don't ask for problems, and we certainly don't want our children to struggle, but problems and struggles will come despite our best wishes.

You might not believe it now, but single mothers can and do grow strong from the challenges they face, and their children can and do emerge from the cocoon of family complete and able to fly. Mother after mother told me with pride of the difficulties overcome, the lessons learned.

I really like that I am responsible for my own messes. I don't have anyone to blame but myself. And when I goof, I forgive myself, and I'm more forgiving of others. And when I succeed, then I feel good about that too. And I can talk with my children about how to solve those problems and recover from mistakes. That's a gift I couldn't give to my kids when I was all wrapped up in the dysfunctional marriage.

Grown-up children of single mothers also described how they use the lessons they learned from living in a single mother household—even the toughest lessons—in their own parenting.

Somehow everyone looked the other way when my mother took on full financial responsibility for raising me. Our lives together would have stung much less, and she would have felt less desperate, if we hadn't been so poor, if she had gone back to school. She might have been able to create her own successes, discover a bud or two of confidence. I was very involved in school and did well academically. I took a lot of pride in this and received a lot of encouragement from my teachers because of it and went on to get a B.A.

I was left alone a lot as a child, and with my children I am very present. I take nothing for granted. Not a sad look, an unfinished homework assignment, an angry shove. I am not a perfect parent. I make announcements at least once a week that I am not the maid. I can be selfish and demanding and critical at times, but I am always, always around. I am protective. I persevere.

This young mother and former daughter of a single mother eloquently articulates what I want to stress throughout this book: single mothers need to take care of themselves—discover and nurture that "bud or two of confidence"—in order to take the best care of their children. Your children notice how you live your life, as a mother and as an independent woman. Teach them well. Let them learn.

TAKE A MINUTE

Lessons Learned

Eleanor Roosevelt said, "You must do the thing you think you cannot do."

Take a minute and think of something you've done (either as a single mother or at some other time in your life) that you thought you could not do.

How did you feel after you accomplished the task or overcame the difficulty? What lesson did you learn?

PARENTING FROM A POSITION OF STRENGTH

Positiveness breeds resilience. We hear so much about the disadvantages of single-parent families and little about the benefits. Yes, single-parent families have problems, but we all know plenty of women and children who thrived in single mother households. Focusing on probable benefits instead of possible deficits helps us parent from a position of strength, not doubt. Here are just some of the positive aspects of single parenting. Add to the list as you think of more.

◾ Single mothers have a wonderful opportunity to model both independence and interdependence to their children. You send an important message about women to both your sons and your daughters when they see you caring for them, balancing work and household responsibilities, and asking for help when you need it. Children of single mothers are not as bound to gender stereotypes because they develop a more positive view of women and a less rigid view of sex roles. As Gloria Steinem once said, "Some of us are becoming the men we wanted to marry." The lessons learned in a single mother household are long-lived, as this grown-up daughter pointed out:

> Even though I have a traditional family of my own now, I still do a lot of things myself that a man might do (which my husband seems to appreciate!). I was given a lot of good advice by my mother, and watching her as a strong woman and single mother gave me strength. I learned you can do anything you set your mind to, that you should be independent but responsible for your own actions.

Daughters and sons of single moms learn that it's okay to be both strong *and* sensitive.

I remember a time when I lost my day-care provider. I was overwhelmed. All the good day cares were always full, and I hated leaving my children with strangers. I sat in my tiny little bathroom and sobbed. My youngest daughter came in, rubbed my back, and said, "Don't cry, Mommy. It's going to be okay." Those beautiful, little, needy children got me—their grown mother—through that moment. I have tears in my eyes now remembering it.

◘ If you are a single mother because of a divorce, things might be calmer now because you and your former spouse are no longer arguing in front of your children or bringing past marital tension into the house. You can be more present with your children and more attendant to their emotional needs when you aren't angry or upset. Also, single parents who aren't distracted by the expectations or time demands of another adult can spend more uninterrupted time with their children.

I asked my daughter last winter what she remembered about when her daddy and I lived together in our old house, and she said, "All the fighting." She had the saddest look on her face.

◘ Children of single mothers can learn much about cooperative living from mothers who involve them in the day-to-day things that go into running a single-parent household. Such learning is usually incremental, starting with manageable tasks that young children can perform and adding on duties as the children get older.

My son and I always cooked dinner together, and then we'd set the table and have a candlelight meal almost every night—just the two of us. He helped out in other ways too but was pretty stubborn when it came to cleaning his room. He'd argue with me, saying things like "Oscar the Grouch [on television's *Sesame Street*] doesn't have to clean *his* room." I told him, "But Oscar lives in a trash can! Your room isn't a trash can—not yet anyway."

Children who grow up with a sense of responsibility make splendid, caring adults and are more likely to be equal partners when they get involved in relationships of their own.

Sometimes one or both my sons would do all of the cleaning when they got home from school on Friday so we could all play on the weekend. That was a real treat!

■ Single mothers who involve themselves and their children in a community help their children develop as confident social beings.

Some of the best memories growing up were summer camping and events with Parents without Partners— setting up tents in rainstorms, New Year's Eve dinners followed by a movie, the great Halloween costumes my mom created every year.

■ Single mothers who seek help when it is needed help their children view assistance from others as a gift, not a weakness.

I worried about the long-term effects the divorce would have on my daughter and sought counseling for both of us early on. The counselor was wonderful and helped both of us make the transition, and my daughter learned that it's okay to talk about her feelings.

In sum, children of single mothers stand a good chance of emerging as nonsexist, compassionate, and responsible adults who recognize the value of education and hard work and who aren't afraid to ask for help when they need it. I'd say this isn't a bad gift to give the world.

I remember only having thirty dollars to buy groceries for the month. We ate a lot of peanut butter sandwiches. But I can say, now that my girls are all grown up, that I did a damn good job by myself. They both graduated from high school. One has a great job, and the other is in college.

Single mothers who approach parenting positively, with a generous dose of consistency and love, have an excellent chance of raising healthy, resilient children.

We lived in the projects and didn't have much of anything, but my friends at school never acted snobbish towards us. In fact, they would rather come and stay at my house with me than have me come to their houses, because my mom was so much fun. My mom had a lot of struggles and hardships as a single mother of five, but she never let on to us. I am a mother of four now, and I have a husband who loves his family and is as involved in our children's lives as I am. My mom really influenced the way I parent, and my relationship with her is still great. My kids adore her.

TOWARD POSITIVE PARENTING

In his book *Lost Boys*, James Garbarino defines resiliency as "the ability to bounce back from crisis and overcome stress and injury." He said that to be resilient, children need spiritual, psychological, and social "anchors" that connect them to positive values and relationships. Spiritual anchors give deeper meaning to their lives and help them sort through the tough questions like "Who am I?" Psychological anchors include authentic self-esteem, constructive coping strategies, intellectual ability, the capacity to actively respond to events rather than passively react to them, an ability to seek social support from outside the family, and having someone who is crazy about them. Social anchors are found in the social health of families, schools, and communities and include adults who commit themselves unconditionally to meeting a child's developmental needs.

We've already talked about the importance of a supportive community and the benefits of having caring and committed mentors in both your and your children's lives. These relationships tether our children to the positive values and environment we seek to construct for them. These support systems should be encouraged and nurtured, but they are supplements to, not replacements for, good healthy parenting.

In *Self-Esteem: A Family Affair,* Jean Illsley Clarke emphasizes that self-esteem, an essential ingredient in resilience, starts at home. Living with positive self-esteem, she says, doesn't take any more time or energy than living with low self-esteem. We feed our children's positive self-esteem first and foremost by modeling it. Clarke tells parents to "Love yourself, appreciate your accomplishments, accept your mistakes, and change them without beating on yourself. Find some other people who will swap that kind of healthy relationship with you." She says to claim the things you are doing well as a parent and identify the areas in which you need to improve. Then get help if you need it.

Practicing positive parenting builds your own self-esteem, feeds your children's self-esteem, and builds resilience in you and your children. There is no one way to raise children, and it's not necessary for you to have received good parenting in your family in order to parent successfully. The goal is to create a safe place for your children without smothering them or abandoning them. Family therapists call these two extremes enmeshment and disengagement.

MOTHERING NOT SMOTHERING: ESTABLISHING APPROPRIATE BOUNDARIES

My daughter will be the first one to point out that I have been an overprotective parent. In the early days of single motherhood I found it especially hard to know where I ended and Jessica began. Things balanced out more when I remarried a wonderful parenting partner, but some of the hovering habits I had established during those first years when Jessica and I lived alone were hard to shake. Even now when she is an adult, the mother lion in me frequently roars up and gnaws away the parent/child boundaries I try to maintain. When I slip into the realm of no boundaries or blurred boundaries, we become an "enmeshed" family. Other families might be "disengaged," with rigid boundaries and members who think isolation and detachment are normal.

It is normal for families to dance along the continuum from enmeshment to disengagement as we and our children go through various ages and stages. The ideal is to establish clear boundaries with your children somewhere in the middle ground of enmeshment and disengagement. Children need to feel safe and secure, especially if there has been a dramatic change in the family structure because of divorce or death. They're hurting, and it's natural to want to shield them from all other pain. But the best we can do is love them and reassure them that we are there for the long haul. The ultimate goal is to nurture strong and independent children, and we do this best by striking a balance. We learn the subtle difference, as one poem says, "between holding a hand and chaining a soul."

> I like that I get to set boundaries and negotiate the rules with my kids and create a safe place for them in my home. I like that I get to talk and feel my way with them when we work through difficult issues, like when my son head butted another kid, or what to do with our anger (which we both have at times), or how they feel about the divorce.

We differentiate ourselves from others by setting appropriate boundaries. Boundaries protect and preserve our individuality and help us maintain positive self-esteem.

Take a Minute

Enmeshed or Disengaged?

Take a minute to consider where on the enmeshment-disengagement continuum you usually operate.

If your child came home from school brokenhearted over a fight with a friend, would your tendency be to intervene in some way and try to fix the friendship, or would you brush off the incident and tell your child to get over it?

Taking on someone else's problems or pain as your own could be a symptom of enmeshment. Dismissing or discounting someone's feelings or concerns could signal disengagement.

Are there things you could do in the above example that would convey support and understanding while helping your child find her or his own solution?

PARENTING AS A PRACTICE

When I teach writing, I use writer Natalie Goldberg's analogy and remind my students that writing is a continual practice, like running or Zen meditation. The more you do it, the better you get. You learn to trust your instincts and ability, and practice, practice, practice. You write junk, you make mistakes, you start over, you keep going. And then one day when you aren't even looking, you're writing smoothly. All the rules and tips you struggled to remember are now woven in so deeply you aren't even conscious of using them.

Parenting is a continual practice too, and parents, like writers, have different styles. Some parents are restrictive and more authoritarian, often more concerned with their own needs for order and obedience than their children's needs or desires. There is little or no negotiating or problem solving with children in this style of parenting. These parents are more disengaged, with very rigid boundaries.

On the other end of the spectrum are the permissive, enmeshed parents who are inconsistent with discipline or rules because they are too easily swayed by the needs or desires of their children. Boundaries are blurred or nonexistent.

As was the case with boundaries, it's good to aim for the middle ground, being responsive to your children's needs, but making it clear that you are their parent, not their peer. Set age-appropriate limits and boundaries, but be willing to bend and negotiate if they have a valid position. Responsive parents are able to be warm and supportive even when they have to enforce consequences for inappropriate behavior.

Motherhood is not an exact science, and what works one time may not work every time, because we and our children change from year to year, from experience to experience. Harriet Lerner, the author of the national best-seller *The Mother Dance,* urges mothers to be patient with themselves. "When anxiety is high enough, or lasts long enough, even the most supercreative mothers hit rock bottom," writes Lerner. "Of course you will lose it, yell at your kid, and get stuck in too much distance, intensity, and blame. You will set rules and consequences and fail to follow through, on the one hand, or you will be too rigid and inflexible, on the other. You will do these things not because you're a bad mother but because you are a human being."

We hear the phrase "maternal instinct" bandied about like it's some mutant gene imbedded in our hormones that will miraculously be released with the last push of labor or as soon as we've signed our name on the dotted line on the adoption papers. If we don't instinctively know how to act like a mother, we worry that something must be wrong with us. Here again, parenting is like writing. Some students take to writing more easily than others, but none of them gets good at it without practice and hard work. In *Operating Instructions,* a funny and poignant journal of her son's first year, single mother Anne Lamott writes of motherhood with a self-effacing honesty that gets us all off the hook when it comes to maternal instinct. "It feels like I'm baby-sitting in the *Twilight Zone.* I keep waiting for the parents to show up because we're out of chips and Diet Cokes. . . . I really had no idea what I was getting into. To tell you the truth, I thought it would be more like getting a cat."

It's comforting to know that there are parents out there who are even more uncertain than we are about the mysteries of child rearing. Single mothers do not have to parent in a vacuum. There are good resources available to guide parents through the various stages of child development. Use the resource list at the back of this book as a launching pad to discover the wealth of information at your fingertips (page 168). In addition, many community education departments offer special classes for parents and children.

The National Association for the Education of Young Children (www.naeyc.org) has a complete list of places that offer accredited Early Childhood Family Education (ECFE) classes. A typical ECFE session begins with time for parents and their children from birth to kindergarten to enjoy classroom activities together. Then, children play and learn under the supervision of a licensed early childhood teacher, while parents share child-rearing experiences and ideas with other parents and a licensed parent educator. Classes like this are another opportunity for families from different income levels and backgrounds to connect around their common concerns as parents. They are a great way to build community while setting the stage for a positive K–12 educational experience.

Practice, practice, practice. And when your child reaches another stage of development, practice some new parenting skills. According to various child development experts such as Dr. James Herzog, senior scholar in child psychiatry at Harvard Medical School, your main job with a newborn is to make your baby feel loved and secure. Talk and sing softly, show him or her pictures and colors, introduce new textures and sounds that stimulate the child's brain. Herzog says that at about eight months, your child is able to form a mental picture of you, so he or she can be "with you" even when you need to be apart.

Mothers and children find ways to balance dependence and independence during the first two years of a child's life. Things change fast for your toddler, and it's important not to minimize the loss of babyhood with reprimands like "Don't be a baby," or "Only babies do that." Instead, sympathize a little but be positive about the wonderful toys and children at preschool and other things that lie ahead. Little rewards that encourage mature behavior work well with toddlers. Herzog advises mothers to keep up their friendships and activities so their babies will realize they don't satisfy all their mothers' needs. Caregivers with predictable routines can lessen separation anxiety. It will also help if you stay calm and keep your good-byes short and comforting when you need to be apart.

As your children go out into the world of school and new experiences, they begin the difficult but exciting process of becoming less dependent on you. It is their job to move into their own skin, their own personalities. And it is your job to help them let go. They will test you and try you, and there will be mood swings as they do the dance from intimacy to loss with you, with their friends, and with their childhood. It's normal for your teens to feel sad over the changes and disappointments they will encounter, but if their sadness turns to self-blame and hopelessness, they may need to get help for depression. This adult child of a single mother—now a mother herself—remembered the feelings she had as a child:

> I think I was pretty depressed as a kid. But I was just so good, no one noticed. By the time I became a teenager, I was angry and hurt at being so ignored—so I began to use drugs and drink a very small amount. I never became a heavy user because it made me feel sick and more depressed. I still struggle with depression and have been in various therapies since I was twenty-nine. I should have been in therapy when I was a kid, but neither of my parents had any real knowledge or experience with therapy and up until I became an explosive teenager, I did everything I was supposed to do. I didn't create enough trouble for anyone to consider how I was feeling.

If children are depressed, it does no good to join in their despair or try to talk them out of their feelings. The best you can do is acknowledge their feelings and help them take some action that can make them feel better. You are the soft but firm shoulder on which they seek refuge. Notice and celebrate their achievements and encourage and comfort them when they need support. Most important, keep the doors of communication open.

COMMUNICATION IS THE KEY

A recent public service announcement on television called communication the "anti-drug." While being able to talk openly and honestly with your children is no guarantee that they will grow up drug- and trouble-free, establishing healthy communication in your home is another way to build their resilience so they will be better able to withstand the pressures of peers and society and make responsible choices. As National Family Partnerships says in the publication "Parenting Is Prevention": "If the foundation of prevention is good parenting, then the heart of good parenting is communication. We can't talk to our kids about drugs if we're not first listening to them talk about what's important to them."

Talking with our kids takes practice and patience, as this mother and grown daughter of a single mother points out:

> I have spent hours with my children discussing the existence of hell or God or what beauty means; why telling the truth matters; why a democracy needs protestors; why being hurt looks a lot like being angry; or which friend said what; and how my children want to be a teacher, a photographer, a dancer, an artist, a scientist, a writer, an actress, an archeologist. I have listened to mind-numbing daily reports on gym class or silly jokes told outside the locker area. So many of these discussions took place not at all or only with friends or the occasional baby-sitter when I was a child.

Ideally, you will develop an open-door communication policy with your children so they will feel comfortable talking to you about anything and everything.

> When my cousin got terminal cancer, she didn't think she could talk to her boys about it. Then a friend reminded her, "If you can put a condom on a banana and

talk about safe sex with them, you can talk about the cancer." She realized that was true. There was nothing they couldn't discuss.

It's taken me many years of practice and many classes in interpersonal communication to learn how to put feelings into words. Identifying my feelings was tough enough; expressing them seemed unfathomable. Before my divorce, I remember feeling paralyzed when a marriage counselor asked me what I was feeling. "Show me then," he urged. "Stand up and show me where you are in this relationship." I moved in slow motion, got up, walked to the farthest corner of the room, turned my back to my husband and the therapist, and covered my eyes with my hands. I am forever grateful that this insightful psychologist gave me a way to express myself when I could not find words to articulate my despair and loneliness. "Now come back and try to tell us how you feel." This simple exercise loosened me up, and the words began to flow with the tears.

This is what we can do for our children. By helping them identify and talk about their feelings, they learn that it's okay to feel whatever emotion they are feeling and that it's good to use language to get their feelings out so they won't be tempted to cover them up with drugs or alcohol, stuff them with food or isolation, or release them inappropriately through aggression or violence.

My kids are too little for sophisticated or reflective discussions, so we made a chart to help them talk about feelings. We found pictures of animals or people or scenes that looked happy, confused, sad, angry, and so on. Then we cut them out, pasted them on poster board, and labeled the feelings accordingly. It was fun! Each day after supper, we get the chart out to identify our feelings or experiences of the day.

After we find the words that best describe our feelings, it helps to practice expressing ourselves by saying "I feel

_____ because _____." This process links emotions to thought and helps us talk about the feeling and the reason for the feeling.

Volumes have been written on how to communicate, and while techniques may vary from author to author, they inevitably underscore the importance of listening. It takes practice and patience to become a "listening presence," but no skill is as valuable when it comes to communicating with children. So much of what they really want and need to say often gets lodged in the cracks of their seeming chitchat, and if you learn to listen attentively, you help them get at what they need and want to talk about.

This form of listening is sometimes called mirroring. When we mirror accurately, children know they are being taken seriously. We validate their emotions and send them the message that we respect them as individuals with individual feelings and thoughts. When you mirror, you clarify what you are hearing by saying in your own words your understanding of what your child is trying to say. You do not parrot their words; you give back your interpretation. For example, if your daughter announces, "I think I'll quit swimming! We waste so much time, and the coach is mean," you might respond with, "You feel like quitting because you think things aren't run well?" Your daughter might then say, "I'm really discouraged. I never feel like I'm good enough." This allows both of you to take the conversation to a deeper level so she can discuss what is really bothering her.

It is important to stay physically present as well when you listen to your child.

> My daughter came home brimming with the news of her day and wanting to tell me about it. She started talking, and I listened, but in the midst of the conversation, I got up to get a glass of water and said over my shoulder, "Go on. I'm listening." All of a sudden, she stomped off

with a "Never mind. Just forget it," and the moment and opportunity were lost.

As Harriet Lerner reminds us, "The challenge is to listen with an open heart and mind, and to ask good questions rather than to rush in to soothe, fix, advise, criticize, instruct, admonish, and do whatever else we do naturally that shuts down the lines of communication." When we try to fix things, we are usually trying to get our children to change to our way of thinking, rather than hearing what they have to say.

When people are listened to well, they tend to listen to themselves with more care and make a greater attempt to express themselves clearly about what they are thinking and feeling. By attentively listening to your child, you convey the idea "I'm interested in you as a person, and I think that what you feel is important. I respect your thoughts, and even if I don't agree with them, I know that they are valid for you. I think you are worth listening to, and I want you to know that you can talk to me." Listening is one of the most effective ways to communicate respect.

Lerner says you can't force your children to communicate with you. Some kids are more comfortable talking when you're in the car or doing dishes together, rather than sitting across from each other, face-to-face, with talking as the sole task at hand. It's important to stay flexible and take advantage of the opportunities whenever and wherever they arise, as this single mother does:

> It was the first Halloween after the divorce, and my son and I were up in the climbing tower in the backyard. He was in his new Spiderman costume, and we had been cuddling. It seemed like a good time to talk about the divorce and reinforce for him that his dad and I would never live in the same house but that he and his sister got to live in two houses and that they didn't ever have to choose who to love because they got to love us both. And then I talked about dating, and my son, disgusted,

slid off my lap and down the slide saying, "Oh, don't do that!" But then he came back up the ladder into the tower, and he talked about how he felt, how he was worried that if one of us got married, the other would no longer be a parent. Scary. We tend to get things clear when we play and talk at the same time.

If most of your communications with your children are negative (such as "Stop running in the house"), your children may feel communication isn't worth it because they're always getting criticized. Positive communication such as "Please walk when you're in the house," or praise such as "Look at how nicely you've picked up your room!" are much more effective than negative dictates.

It is important, however, for children to know what your rules and limits are and that there will be consequences if they break the rules. In the "Parenting Is Prevention" guide, which gives parents tips on how to prevent drug and alcohol abuse, the government's Center for Substance Abuse Prevention advises parents and schools to set clear rules and respond with mild consequences when these rules are broken. The guide says that severe punishments undermine the quality of the parent-child relationship and are no more effective than more moderate, consistently applied consequences.

My daughter knows that no one is allowed to smoke in my car. She borrowed it to go to the basketball game with her friends, and it reeked of cigarettes when I got in to drive it the next morning. She tried to argue at first, but she knew the rule and that she'd lose two weeks of driving privileges each time she broke it. It was an inconvenience to both of us, but it was the last time her friends smoked in my car.

Be as consistent as possible, and be ready to stand behind other agreements you make with your children—especially those that deal with their protection and safety. Work with your children's day-care providers, teachers, therapists, or other qualified adults to develop action plans that your children can follow to keep themselves safe when they are not in your care.

> My ex and I don't communicate very well, and we have different ideas about what constitutes "safe" for the kids. Things happen that I hear about from the kids, but not my ex. Some of it really scares me, and because I'm not there, I can't protect them. There are a number of active alcoholics in my ex's family, and there's a lot of denial about drug and alcohol abuse. My ex is on some kind of medication for ADD that he won't disclose to our kids' therapist, but he's been on other medications before and has gone off as soon as he feels better, saying, "I never really had a problem after all." Sometimes his thinking patterns are pretty crazy. I think the biggest problems might be in finding a way to make the kids safe, teaching them to keep themselves safe, but at the same time, teaching them how to maintain hope and faith in God and in the goodness of other people.

Make sure child-care providers know who is allowed to pick a child up from school or day care, and set clear rules about drinking and driving with any adult who may be transporting your child. Have backup drivers in mind, and let your children know whom to call if they need to find another ride home. The trick is to teach your children practical skills and precautions that will increase their resiliency, not their paranoia. Sometimes you can't anticipate what all this will mean, and you might be forced to put your money where your mouth is, but that's part of parenting too. For instance, we have always had the rule with Jessica that she could call us to get her home if it was unsafe for her to drive or if someone she was with was unable to drive for whatever reason—no questions asked. Her twenty-year-old uncle was killed in an alcohol-related car accident, so we knew all too well about tragic possibilities. She used this "get out of jail free" card a few times in high school when she had us come and get her, giving her friends who had been drinking some excuse like "My parents will go nuts if I'm home late."

All went well until after high school when she was out west with a couple of friends, and the driver was driving erratically. "I'm calling from the Denver airport," she informed us. "Judy and I made Zack drop us off. Can you get us home?" For years we were at-the-ready to retrieve her from a friend's house or a party across town. We were not prepared to buy two plane tickets! But we clicked into high gear, borrowed some money, and got her and her friend safely home. A deal is a deal.

Balance has been the theme throughout this chapter, and communication is also about balance. We might disclose too much or pressure our child to open up if we have an enmeshed family system, or we might avoid a difficult subject entirely or settle for too much distance if our system is disengaged. If we operate at the extremes, we can overreact or underreact to what our child tells us.

There are other common barriers that can get in the way of communicating with your child. If your communication efforts repeatedly break down, ask yourself the following questions, and then try again:

- Am I forgetting to listen to both facts and feelings?
- Do I have a tendency to jump to conclusions?
- Do I frequently give double messages? Are my words saying one thing and my body movements or actions saying something else?
- Am I expecting too much or too little from my child?
- Am I telling my child to do something without allowing her to have a say?
- Am I threatening by holding some punishment over his head?

- Am I preaching by telling my child what she should or ought to do?
- Am I lecturing by talking *to* my child, rather than *with* my child?
- Am I judging my child by criticizing him?
- Am I becoming angry or name calling?
- Am I diverting or avoiding discussion by distracting my child from the problem at hand?

Ultimately, it begins and ends with us. Author Harriet Lerner reminds us that when it comes to us talking to our children, "we won't talk productively to kids about anything we haven't processed ourselves with the relevant adults in our lives. If we don't have a grip on our own emotionality, we will confuse our angry or anxiety-driven responses with 'honesty' and 'open communication.'"

> My son has been having problems with wetting during the day and will hide the fact, even when soaked down to his socks, rather than change into clean, dry clothes. I tried talking to him about having pride and caring for his body, how the other kids could smell the urine, and that he was six years old, and he could learn to not wet, and to change his clothes when he had an accident (and on and on and on). My dad overheard one of these conversations, and he took me aside to tell me that my son obviously felt very bad about the wetting problem and that when things cleared up around the divorce, the wetting would probably disappear. I thought about this and talked about it more at my Al-Anon meeting. That night at bedtime, I said to my son, "I've been really pushing hard about the wetting thing, haven't I?" He said yes, and I said, "I'm sorry. It's just that I keep thinking you should be able to handle this stuff. But you have so much other junk to deal with." My son said, "Mom, you should just tell me to change my clothes and not say

anything else." I told him I would try my best, and if I started lecturing again, he could remind me of my promise. We've been doing good so far. He still wets, but I just tell him to change his clothes and don't lecture him about what he already knows.

So take a deep breath, quiet down, and practice, practice, practice.

Take a Minute

Becoming a Listening Presence

Attentive listening is a skill that allows you to participate in your children's lives without taking over their lives. When you listen attentively, you stay present with the speaker. You focus on what is being said and do not form opinions or prepare responses while listening. You listen without judgment.

Take a minute and practice listening skills with a friend or relative. Set an oven timer for ten minutes and take turns talking while the other person listens attentively. The listener does not jump in at any time to comment or reply; he or she listens respectfully while the speaker talks without interruption.

Was it more difficult for you to listen attentively or to talk without interruption? What did you discover from this exercise?

TEACHABLE MOMENTS

When Kay Provine works with participants in *Roots & Wings**
classes—a program she codeveloped to help parents learn how
to raise resilient children—she uses an AA slogan to remind
them that the goal of parenting is "progress not perfection."
One way to progress toward raising resilient children is to take
advantage of the "teachable moments" that present themselves each day we go about our busy lives.

A teachable moment, she explains, is a moment when our
children are most ready to learn. These moments can be big or
small, anytime something happens to a child that triggers either confusion, curiosity, or conflict. Provine said that such a
moment could involve a mother who gets caught by her children smoking after she has told them not to smoke. By speak-
ing honestly to her children, using "I" statements that address
her feelings and beliefs rather than telling her children how
they should feel or what they should believe, this mother can
use the opportunity to give valuable information to her children and set appropriate expectations.

The mother could tell her children how awful she feels that
they saw her smoking because she knows cigarettes are bad
for her and that they are addictive and make her hair and
clothes smell bad. Provine cautioned that while you want to
give your children accurate information, you should take care
not to scare them or give them more details than are suitable
for their age or level of maturity. The mother could then ask
her children open-ended questions like, "How did it make you
feel when you saw me smoking?" or "What do you think
about this?"

---

* Contact Hazelden Information and Educational Services (800-328-9000) for more
information on the *Roots & Wings* parenting program, or see *What to Say or Do . . .
From Diapers to Diploma* (Hazelden, 2000), a compilation of practical parenting tips
that grew out of the *Roots & Wings* program.

In this example, the mother and children could then settle on some mutual expectations. For instance, the children might voice their desire for their mother to enroll in a class to stop smoking, and the mother might relay her hope that they will use her behavior as a reminder that they should not experiment with cigarettes.

Teachable moments provide good opportunities to practice the communication techniques and listening skills we've already discussed. They are chances to connect with our children on a deeper level, to let them know more about who we are and what we value, and to find out more about who they are and what is important to them. Provine said parents can learn to identify teachable moments by paying attention to their children's faces and body language. If your child's face is scrunched up in confusion or bright with obvious curiosity, or if it's obvious from her body language or his facial expression that your child is having some sort of inner conflict, the time is ripe for a teachable moment. If, however, you are met with blank faces and faraway stares, the lesson would likely be lost at this time.

Years ago, after my husband and daughter and I took part in the first Martin Luther King Jr. birthday march in St. Paul, Minnesota, I received a vile letter from an anonymous person who had read an innocuous quote by me in an article a local reporter wrote about the march. I shook when I opened the envelope filled with white supremacist hate literature and a note that called me "a piece of white vomitous trash" because I had chosen to honor an African American leader. Several friends and their young children happened to be visiting us at the time I received this hate mail, and we used the experience as a teachable moment. We sat in a circle in our living room, and each person had a turn to talk about anger and hate and prejudice. After the discussion, we ceremonially burned the packet in the fireplace and vowed one by one that we would do our best to work for peace and justice.

Ellen Key wrote the words that begin this chapter in 1909, but they still hold true in this new millennium: "At every step the child should be allowed to meet the real experiences of life; the thorns should never be picked from the roses."

Each attempt at connection, each display of compassion, each time we listen respectfully, and each time we take advantage of a teachable moment, we add to the bouquet we present to our children, the skills and tools and lessons we give them that will help them grow resilient and strong so they might truly enjoy the roses.

Take a Minute

Teachable Moments

Take a minute and think of a recent time when your child registered confusion, curiosity, or conflict. Perhaps your son saw you doing something or heard you saying something he had been told not to do or say. Maybe you were taking a walk with your daughter and she saw a street person sleeping in the park and wanted to know why he didn't go home to his own bed. Maybe your child came home obviously agitated over something that happened at school.

What happened? Were there opportunities to talk about your thoughts and feelings and chances to invite your child to talk about his or her thoughts and feelings? Were you able to practice active listening?

Was this experience a teachable moment? If it was not, how could it have become a teachable moment? What was learned or what could have been learned?

SIX

The World Out There

◨ ◨ ◨

> Although the connections are not always obvious, personal
> change is inseparable from social and political change.
> —From *Dance of Intimacy* by Harriet Lerner

EARNING AND LEARNING

Study after study indicates that economic well-being and education have more to do with individual success than family structure. For example, as newspaper writer Lynn Smith reports, in 1997, researchers from the University of Southern California and the University of Washington matched the occupational status of 22,761 men to the family type in which they were raised. They found that those raised by working single moms did nearly as well professionally as those brought up in two-parent homes. The children of unemployed single mothers, however, were more likely to hold the lowest-paying jobs.

The international Save the Children organization reports that children who engage in positive learning activities (such as homework, sports, games, and community projects) usually succeed in school and establish a foundation for future achievement. There is also evidence that a parent's attitude toward and experience with education can influence a child's educational success. According to U.S. Bureau of the Census statistics for 1998, children born to a mom who has less than a high school diploma are twice as likely to drop out of school as the children of a mother who is a high school graduate.

> Many of my elementary students come from single mother homes. I think the stress of making money stretch to meet family needs with only one income can be a tremendous burden that spills into every aspect of life, including a child's adjustment at school. Often, in order to have medical coverage and to meet the economic necessities of the family, the mother must work full-time. Good child care is expensive and takes a big bite out of salaries that are often minimum wage. Educated mothers who are able to hold higher-paying jobs seem to have a huge advantage in raising their children.

Poor children in any family situation—single-parent, two-parent, or no-parent—are at a higher risk when it comes to getting an education and a good-paying job. It's poverty, not parenting that's the culprit, and single mother households bear the brunt of the burden of poverty. According to the Children's Defense Fund's statistics for 2000, 50 percent of America's poor children live in female-headed families. (A three-person family was considered to be poor in 1998 if it made less than $13,003 per year, but the average poor family with children had less than $9,000 of total income.)

> I think the biggest challenge for single moms is money. In my case, and in so many other's that I have seen throughout the years, a newly divorced mom with her kids is always lower on the economic scale than before the divorce. Child support is great if it arrives, but I know so many women who ended up handling everything on their own.

It's tough enough for a single person to make ends meet with today's high cost of housing, health care, and other living expenses. The challenge is even greater for single mothers who also have to feed and clothe their children, pay for expensive day care, buy school supplies, and cover all the other costs of maintaining a household and a family.

> I wish I would have had the foresight to know that I needed a smart lawyer who could write a divorce decree that would protect me in the future. It was never explained to me that I could appeal for an increase in support when my ex's salary increased. I made do for many years on not much child support while my ex-husband ladder-climbed at his job and received a lot more money. The kids and I continued to just scrape by while he bought many new things and took lavish vacations.

Ask another lawyer or your county's legal aid office if you have questions about child support payments, or you can find your state's office of child support enforcement by going to the Federal Office of Child Support Enforcement home page (www.acf.dhhs.gov/programs/cse) or calling the agency in Washington (202-401-9200).

If you, like many single mothers, find yourself in dire financial straits, however temporary, contact your county department that deals with social services to find out what assistance is available to you. They can tell you about government programs such as the federal Temporary Assistance for Needy Families (TANF, which replaced the Aid to Families with Dependent Children [AFDC] program). TANF provides assistance and work opportunities to needy families by granting states the federal funds and flexibility to develop and implement their own welfare programs. In Minnesota, for example, several organizations have teamed up with state agencies in order to help families obtain the financial and support services they need to get them on their feet. Such things as low-interest car loans, work clothes, mentoring, and voice mail are available through some programs, as well as assistance for food and housing.

Helen Keller once said, "Although the world is full of suffering, it is full also of the overcoming of it." Single mothers are proof of this. I've heard story after remarkable story of single mothers who struggled to pull themselves and their children out of poverty, put themselves and their children through school, and, contrary to all myths that would have us believe otherwise, are living happily ever after.

> As a housing manager for subsidized housing, I work with many low-income single mothers of various ethnic and educational backgrounds. We have a self-sufficiency program where a few single mothers have been able to accrue an escrow account, and at the end of their contract, they were able to use the money to make a down payment on a house. I just saw a mother last week who was able to buy her own house. It was fantastic—lots of hugs all around!

Some of these stories remind me of the ones my mother and grandmother would tell me about the Great Depression, when there was not enough money to buy the sugar needed to completely frost a birthday cake. While they didn't want to go back to those days of hardship, they spoke of their experiences with a mixture of pride and gratitude for having endured. And the lessons learned were long lasting. I think my grandmother invented the concept of reuse and recycle, a practice that served me well as a single mother on a tiny budget that I stretched by shopping at garage sales and secondhand stores.

While it's hard to realize it when we're going through the tough times, our children learn important values and build resilience watching us and even helping us overcome hardships, just as I learned from my mother and grandmother. They carry these lessons into adulthood and will pass them on to their children.

I remember that my mom and us five kids always seemed to go to a different house for dinner every night at the end of the month. I thought this was pretty cool, and I remember that my cousins actually envied us because we got to go visit people more than they did. As I got older, I realized the reason for the visiting was because we didn't have any food of our own, and the food stamps weren't due for at least a week. Mom never let on how bad things were and always made the best of any situation. She gave us a happy childhood.

Keeping a detailed record of your income and expenses can help you track and control your spending. List the money you take in each month from salary, child support, and public assistance. Then record the average you spend each month on things like rent, household expenses, child care, food, clothing, car expenses, insurance, entertainment, and other miscellaneous items for you and your children. If your expenses are greater than your income, look at ways you can save money. Can you eat more meals at home? Can you take the bus or carpool more often? Can you barter with other single mothers for child care or other services? Can you shop at your local consignment shop? Can you cut back on entertainment?

Be especially cautious about using your ATM and credit cards so you won't have any unwelcome surprises at the end of the month when your statements arrive. It's easy to forget to record the money you withdraw from a cash machine, and it's hard to keep track of credit card charges. ATM fees can add up. A fee of just $3 a week, for example, would total $156 at the end of the year. That might not sound like a lot, but if you invested that amount in a mutual fund at 10 percent interest, you could save $5,241 in fifteen years.

As challenging as budgeting can be, there is a certain satisfaction that comes with being in control of your own life and finances.

We didn't have a lot of money during our marriage, but my ex spent a lot anyway and created a lot of credit card debt. I'd cringe every time I heard him say, "Look what I got today." I liked being able to control my own money after the divorce. Sure, I would splurge once in a while, but it felt more within my financial grasp. I managed through some very difficult times, which increased my self-confidence and willingness to take risks. Being responsible for myself and my children gave me the courage to take the steps I needed to take.

I heard somewhere that courage is fear that has said its prayers. Providing food, shelter, love, and safety for you and your children can be a frightening prospect. Spinning fear into courage takes trust, hard work, and help, but with time, single moms can outspin Rumpelstiltskin. They are some of the most courageous people I've seen.

TAKE A MINUTE

Preparing a Monthly Budget

If you're like me, "budget" is a four-letter word that conjures up images of coupons and calculators. Maybe it's because I was once married to an accountant, but my shoulders get tense when I start thinking in terms of debits and credits, assets and liabilities.

Resistant as I am to the idea of a budget, I do, nevertheless, recognize its value, and I do try to track our income and expenses each month. A budget is a blueprint for smart living. It can help you get a handle on where your money is going and where it needs to go.

Take a minute and prepare a budget by estimating what you spend each month (divide annual expenditures by twelve). Try to be as accurate as possible.

Housing

House payment or rent	$ _____
Monthly taxes (if applicable)	$ _____
Homeowner's or renter's insurance	$ _____
Gas	$ _____
Electric	$ _____
Water	$ _____
Garbage	$ _____
Telephone (include long distance)	$ _____
Internet service	$ _____
Cable TV	$ _____
Furniture and appliances	$ _____
Repairs and maintenance	$ _____
TOTAL HOUSING COSTS:	$ _____

Transportation

Car payment	$ _____
Auto insurance	$ _____
Gasoline	$ _____
Car license	$ _____
Average monthly maintenance	$ _____
Public transportation costs	$ _____
Parking	$ _____
TOTAL TRANSPORTATION COSTS:	$ _____

Clothing

For yourself	$ _____
For child no. 1	$ _____
For child no. 2	$ _____
For child no. 3	$ _____
Miscellaneous	$ _____
TOTAL CLOTHING COSTS:	$ _____

Groceries, etc.

Food	$ _____
Paper goods, detergents, etc.	$ _____
Pharmaceutical items	$ _____
TOTAL GROCERY COSTS:	$ _____

Entertainment

Movies, concerts, etc.	$ _____
Restaurants	$ _____
Children's entertainment	$ _____
Club memberships	$ _____
Vacation costs	$ _____

Video rentals $ _____

Other entertainment $ _____

TOTAL ENTERTAINMENT COSTS: $ _____

Health Care

Medical premiums $ _____

Dental $ _____

Glasses, etc. $ _____

Other medical expenses $ _____

TOTAL HEALTH CARE COSTS: $ _____

Child Care

Regular day-care expenses $ _____

Baby-sitting costs $ _____

TOTAL CHILD-CARE COSTS: $ _____

School

For yourself (include tuition, books, etc.) $ _____

For your children $ _____

TOTAL SCHOOL COSTS: $ _____

Miscellaneous

Toys $ _____

Gifts, cards $ _____

Pets $ _____

Newspapers and magazines $ _____

Anything else $ _____

TOTAL MISCELLANEOUS COSTS: $ _____

TOTAL MONTHLY EXPENSES: $ _____

Now, *take a minute* and list your income.

Income

Monthly salary	$ _____
Child support	$ _____
Dividends, interest	$ _____
Public assistance	$ _____
Gifts, bonuses	$ _____
Other income	$ _____
TOTAL INCOME:	$ _____
MONTHLY BALANCE	
(subtract expenses from income)	$ _____

How does the money you take in each month stack up against the money you spend? Are there any adjustments that you can make? How you choose to spend your money on a day-to-day basis can make a significant difference over time.

WORKING OUTSIDE THE HOME

Being a single mom brought out an entrepreneurial side of myself I didn't know existed. Jessica was just three months old when I separated from my former husband, and I dreaded the thought of leaving her to go back to work full-time. I wanted to find a way to have a flexible work schedule, go to school when I could afford it, and have time to be with my baby as much as I could. That's when I teamed up with my friend and former coworker Pat, who was also a single mother. Her son was just a year older than Jessica, and she struggled with the same time, money, work, and child-care dilemmas I did. We had worked together in a small law firm where we were everything from receptionists to bookkeepers to legal assistants. I can't remember which one of us first said, "Let's start an employment service." I do remember we approached the endeavor like Spanky and his gang when one of the children would gleefully announce, "Let's put on a show for the neighborhood."

We knew nothing about running a business, but we knew a lot about running a law office, and we used that knowledge to launch Cindy and Pat, Legal Assistants. We created an advertising blurb that looked like a legal document, hoping this disguise would get it to the lawyers' desks instead of being tossed out as junk mail by some efficient receptionist. We said we had bookkeepers, bill collectors, process servers, receptionists, and secretaries for hire on an hourly basis. The tactic worked, and calls started coming in. "If we can't find someone, we'll come ourselves," we reassured prospective clients. Of course, there was only the two of us. We were able to control our schedules and could frequently work at home transcribing tapes or making collection calls. We supported ourselves and our children and felt confident and in control of our own lives. It was wonderful working with someone who required no explanation or apology when I wanted to be with my baby or when I needed time off for some other reason. Although our business disbanded when I remarried and moved, both Pat and I have managed to work for ourselves in one way or another since our days of "Cindy and Pat" twenty-five years ago.

Balancing the demands of your job with your responsibilities at home can be tricky, but more companies are becoming family friendly as they learn what it takes to hold on to good employees. Many employers offer paid annual sick leave, flextime, job-sharing, and telecommuting. Consult with the human resources department at your office, or ask your union representative to see what options you have or what arrangements might be possible at your workplace.

If you have worked for at least a year for a company with at least fifty employees, you are probably covered by the federal Family and Medical Leave Act (FMLA), which provides twelve weeks of unpaid leave each year for family needs, including new babies, adoption, and serious illnesses. (Call the U.S. Department of Labor at 800-959-FMLA for more information.) Also check your state's family and medical leave laws to see what other protection you may have.

Get creative at your place of employment and talk with other working parents to develop strategies and work options that ease conflicts between work and family. See if you can use flex-time or some other arrangement so you can attend parent-teacher conferences or school events. See if you can use your sick days to care for a sick child. Be open to compromise and remain sensitive to your coworkers who do not have children. Try to suggest solutions that are fair to all employees, and to your boss. Expect—even demand—equity. Don't expect special privileges.

Work with your children's school or your community social service agency to explore child-care possibilities for before and after school. Some parents who have children in latchkey situations do have other options.

Often children are left alone at an early age for periods of time because a mother cannot afford day-care expenses. One of my six-year-old students asked if I could come home with him because he was afraid. He said he was alone until his mom came home at seven o'clock. She told him not to go outside when she wasn't there, so he said he watched TV and ate peanut butter sandwiches until she came home. This was a caring, loving mother who felt she had no other option. My county has guidance counselors in each school to provide support and groups for children in divorce situations and for those experiencing anger or other problems. We also have a latchkey program at our school for before- and after-school care. Once I became aware of this family's situation, I could connect them to services that would help them out.

Use the resource list you developed in chapter 2 to have friends or relatives in place to call if your child is sick or if there is any emergency at school that you cannot tend to immediately. Don't expect your children's teachers or school to be a surrogate parent at such times.

Be an advocate for yourself and your children, and don't automatically accept that the answer is no, even when that is someone's initial response. Keep your sense of humor, because bureaucracies usually take themselves way too seriously, and humor can disarm even the stodgiest of bureaucrats. Develop staying power and remember that slow glaciers grind down mountains.

Finally, remember to take the time to vote for people and programs that work to protect single mothers and their children. Families need good, affordable childcare, family-friendly workplaces, jobs and training programs, affordable health care, stiffer child-support payment enforcement, child development and parenting classes in high schools and in the community, supportive and well-structured schools, after-school programs for children and teens, good prevention programs, and programs for young people in trouble. Do your homework and vote for positive changes. Our children's futures depend on it.

IT'S NEVER TOO LATE TO GO BACK TO SCHOOL

I am a perpetual student. It took me eighteen years to get my bachelor's degree and another seven to get a master's degree. That means that I've been going to school, on and off, for almost half my life.

I started this educational quest when I was a single mother and Jessica was an infant. I found out about a tuition-assistance program for women and was able to attend the University of Minnesota. Then I found out about competency-based education, where I could test out in certain subjects and get college credit from my local community college for knowledge and experience I had already gained. I got science credits for what I had learned as a community activist fighting nuclear power; I got physical education credits for yoga; I got speech credits for the volunteer teaching I had done; I got communication credits for the writing I had done on our community newspaper; and I got credits for the experience I had gained working many years in a law office. When I passed the requisite tests to prove that I had a working knowledge of these subjects, I had two years' worth of college credit—enough to enter another local university as a junior. I received more assistance there and was able to design a flexible course of study that incorporated some classes where I worked independently with professors so I wouldn't have to go to class. That way, I was able to work, take care of Jessica, and study at night.

School opened me up to a world of words and ideas I

hadn't known was there. I devoured books and discussions, and each time I passed a test or had some success in a class, I stood a little straighter, walked a little more assuredly into the future. Many of the single mothers I heard from echoed my feelings.

> I got an associate's degree in graphic design from a community college after I became a single mother. I was on welfare and in a program called Reach Up where I found that I could get grants to go to college part-time. I took two classes at a time and worked twenty hours a week at a work-study program at the college. It was hard. It was a lot of work. I would often have to stay up late and study after a long day of classes, work, and dealing with demanding kids. I enjoyed learning and discovered that I was not stupid. I felt like I was working toward a goal that would help me and my kids in the future.

Another single mother told me how she started community college when her daughter was two. She got her associate's degree in liberal arts there and was given a scholarship to finish her four-year degree. She got her bachelor's degree when her daughter turned six, then went on to get a law degree five years later.

> The hardest part was the expense of day care and finding time to study. It was a challenge to find a part-time job with a living wage, cover the high cost of medical and dental coverage, and still have quality time with my daughter. But it all worked out. I ran for public office in 1989, when my daughter was fourteen years old, and she gave one of the nominating speeches. She told the delegates, "My mom has always been there for me, and she'll always be there for you too." I still get teary-eyed when I think about it.

Busy single moms who go back to school have to get creative about carving out time to study.

I went back to school as a single mom. Time was precious, and I always carried a schedule with me. I studied while waiting at dentists' offices, ortho appointments, and at football practices. Multitasking was a skill I became very proficient at. My books became part of my appendages. I realized my son would not necessarily know the difference between me sitting down to pay bills, writing a letter, or studying. I told my then seven-year-old that when I put a certain purple bandanna around my neck that I would be studying and would need him to be very, very quiet. The first time I put the purple bandanna on, he was indeed very, very quiet—standing right next to me! We both got good about letting each other know when we need space. Now it's his turn. He's a sophomore at college. I'm working two jobs (and taking a lot of vitamins) to put him through school, but it's all worth it.

College may not be for you, but there are many ways to stretch your mind. My local community education department offers a number of courses on things such as computers, exercise, writing, language, music, gardening, cooking, and crafts. Bookstores and libraries have book clubs. Our science museum has classes for both adults and children.

If you do want to explore college opportunities, the Federal Student Aid Information Center (800-433-3243) is a good place to start. Also check your local community, vocational, and state colleges to see what programs and tuition assistance are available.

Mothers who enjoy learning have a good chance of raising children who will love to learn. It's a good lesson to keep in mind.

SEX AND THE SINGLE MOM

As Andrea Engber and Leah Klungness (*The Complete Single Mother*) remind their readers, "You are single, not dead." There will come a time (believe it or not) when your hormones will kick in, and you will start thinking about sex and dating and love relationships. Take your time. Don't confuse horniness and loneliness with romantic love and rush into a relationship that isn't a good one for you and your children. Most of you have been there and done that, so go slowly this time around.

> Loneliness was not new to me as a single mother, because I was so lonely when I was married. Being single made it okay to seek companionship, but I still had to give myself permission to go and find someone to watch the kids. Loneliness (or maybe it's a need to be loved) can actually motivate people to do things they normally would not do.

If you are a single mother because of a divorce or the death of your spouse, give yourself enough time to adequately grieve your loss, sort out your feelings, and reflect on your own life and the lives of your children. I urge all single moms, whether or not they started out single or were in a partnership before they became single moms, to get comfortable with who they are as independent, strong women before they start dating. Enjoy the awareness that worthiness, attractiveness, and self-esteem are not given to you by another person, but qualities that come from within yourself. You don't *need* someone else to make you whole. That way, when you choose to start dating, you'll do so as a complete and independent individual ready to meet other healthy individuals.

> I've been a single mother for almost two years, but I haven't started dating yet. In my naïveté, I figure I'll only date when the kids are not with me, and I'll be

watching closely to see whether the guy gets along with kids in general, without being controlling. If he's not good, healthy "dad" material, he won't meet the kids, and he won't last long with me either. And if he doesn't respect me, then out he goes. I'm not making that mistake again.

We're social beings and enjoy being in the company of other adults. And we're sexual beings with sexual desires. Although single motherhood is often a case of too many hormones and too little time, you do deserve to have a personal life of your own, to be with your friends, and to date.

The chances are good that if you feel good about yourself, do things you love to do, pursue your own interests through groups, clubs, or classes, and accept invitations of friends to join them in group activities, you will meet new people and potential dates. If you don't know the person well, the first date should be in a public place. If possible, meet for lunch during the workday so you can avoid baby-sitting costs and have a good excuse to leave if it isn't going well.

Be honest with your date about your children. When I met men as a single mom, I confess that my honesty bordered on rudeness. I'd often begin a conversation with an interested man by saying, "I'm divorced and have a baby girl. Do you still want to get to know me?" It was a crude but effective time-saver that I don't necessarily recommend.

Unless and until a romantic relationship develops, there is no reason to involve your children in your dating life. No matter how casual the date is, children often worry that their lives and their relationship with you will be changed by this person.

My children never met one other person I dated except the man I married, and they liked him. I wasn't about to introduce my children to some man I hardly knew.

Try to schedule first dates when your children are at a sitter's or at their dad's for visitation. If you continue to date this person, gradually introduce your children by doing family-oriented activities together.

> When I began dating after my divorce, I usually didn't introduce my dates to my kids. I never hid the fact that I was a single mom, but I just didn't want my kids getting confused with my different dates. I didn't date too many different people, but only when I became pretty serious did I let my kids in on our times together. My second husband happened to be a close family friend, so when we began seriously dating, it was a pretty easy transition for the kids. They already liked him.

Introduce the person you're dating to your children simply as your friend. Expect your children to be polite when you introduce them to your date, but don't pressure them to like your new friend. Your children would probably like it best if you didn't date at all, because they may not want to share you with anyone. They might be angry, jealous, resentful, or sad when they see you moving on with your life. Respond with love, understanding, and open communication, but don't let their reactions control your actions. Explain to them that you need adult friends just as they need and want friends in their lives. This adult daughter (now a mother herself) remembers when her single mom dated:

> My mother didn't date a whole lot. She did have one man she was seeing when I was about thirteen. I hated him with a passion. I was mean and rude anytime he would come over and threatened to run away many times if he continued to date my mom. I spent most of that summer at my cousin's house. I didn't want to go home if there was a chance my mom's boyfriend was there. I remember taking long walks down this dirt road with my cousin. There was a sign on a tree, and I would pretend that it was my mother's boyfriend's face and throw rocks at it. Now looking back, it wasn't that I

really hated him. I hated the idea of my mom replacing us with someone else.

Be discreet about a sexual relationship, especially if you choose to have casual sex with someone with whom you do not want a long-term relationship. As Engber and Klungness point out, this may be a time of experimentation for you or "the first time you ever felt 'the earth move' even though the guy may possess the IQ of an eggplant." This is your business, not your children's. Do practice safe sex, however, if you choose to have sex. Give yourself the same talking to you'd give your teenage children or your best girlfriend, and follow your own advice about protection and privacy.

> I became a single parent when I left an abusive relationship. I was celibate for six years after I left, because I was afraid to get involved with anyone for fear it would turn abusive and be too painful. I found out I could make it on my own, and that was empowering. I did not want to give up my autonomy, which was what I thought would happen if I got involved with someone. Then one summer I went on vacation, and I was determined to have sex before the vacation ended. I met a guy through friends. I liked him a lot and was very attracted to him, and we're both musicians. We've been together since then.

Continue to maintain appropriate boundaries as a relationship develops, to protect both your children and your lover from forming strong attachments to each other that may cause them pain if the relationship doesn't work out. Don't expect your lover to be a parent to your children by assigning this person child-care or other parenting responsibilities. Let whatever will happen, happen as slowly and naturally as possible.

> I had one serious relationship with a guy who was almost a live-in. My children were crazy about him, and it

was an emotional disaster for all of us when the relationship ended. I learned the difficult lesson that children make independent and equally important relationships with their mom's lover, assuming that he or she is as terrific as he or she should be. So when the deal busts, the parent suffers and has to deal with another loss for herself and for her children. I was very honest with my kids about everything (dating, sex, upheavals, hopes), which may have been too much for them at the time, but I believe it contributed to our closeness. If I had been a bit more affluent, I think I would have gone away with lovers rather than having them around. But it wasn't an option. My children liked my fellows, but were totally clear about the fact that they didn't want any stepsisters or brothers. "No 'patched' households," they said. That was their bottom line.

Use good judgment about what you discuss with your children. Some single mothers make the mistake of treating even young children as confidants. Children can suffer from information overload and often end up worrying unnecessarily about their parents.

On a recent plane trip, my seat companion was a nine-year-old girl who happily filled me in on all her summer plans and her problems as a child of single parents. She said her mom might lose her job because "they tell lies about her at work." She lamented about her dad's girlfriends, saying her dad always picks women who are "like teenagers." She seemed very worried about her parents' jobs and love lives.

If a relationship reaches the stage of serious commitment, be open and honest about your feelings and encourage your children to be open and honest about theirs. If communication becomes strained or impossible, consider family and individual counseling so you, your children, and your prospective partner will have a safe place to share your concerns. Even adult children have difficulty picturing their mom with a new partner.

> My mom was serious with one man she dated, and she asked us each how we'd feel if she remarried. Two of us said okay; two of us said we didn't like the idea. I was a no vote. I felt she could do better. She turned him down. They are still friends, and I think she feels she made the right choice.

Try to keep your relationship with a significant other in balance with your relationship with and obligations to your children. It's hard for everyone if children feel they have to compete with their mother's lover for her time.

> I think my mother's boyfriends saw me as an intruder or a rival. To have a parent decide to live with some love interest is like being banished in one's own home for a child. I dealt with this problem by cultivating an elaborate fantasy and passion for flight. I was running away, in some form, from the time I was nine years old.

If a love relationship has unfolded gradually and healthily, with you and your partner communicating openly and honestly (and appropriately) with your children, it will not be a surprise if you decide to move in together or marry. Ideally, your children will have had the time to form their own relationship with your partner. My husband knew that he wanted to marry me, but he was not sure if he was ready to take on instant fatherhood. I can still remember the moment when he realized he loved Jessica as well as me. We were eating broccoli pie, and Jessica, just a toddler, was delightfully giggling as she smeared the colorful mess all over her face and high chair. Michael grinned at her, then me, and just said, "Let's do it. Let's get married." That was twenty-seven years ago, and we've been a family ever since.

Not all remarriages have this happy ending, however. We were lucky. My former husband has not been a part of our lives, and Michael was able to adopt Jessica a year after we were married. But some children never warm up to their stepparents, and some stepparents don't form a close bond with a mother's children.

> I don't think my children much like the person I married, but they've always been supportive of me and my decisions. It's not ideal but still the best of the available choices. It's all been quite forthright. The children are grown now and living independently, but we are still very connected.

Poet Renee Duvall wrote that "Marriage is the art of balancing the desires of each within the hearts of both and doing so without uneven sacrifice to either." When single mothers marry, that definition grows as mother, partner, and children attempt to balance their desires and feelings without "uneven sacrifice" to anyone.

Take a Minute

Developing Your Dating Criteria

Dating might seem as foreign a concept to you as space travel right now, but thinking about it ahead of time can save you time, energy, and heartache in the long run. I think it's a good idea to be as clear about what you will not tolerate in a date as what you would find desirable. Stay away from violent, abusive, and disrespectful people with obvious drug or alcohol dependencies. Avoid those who dislike children. Know what's important to you. How important are a person's values, religion, political preferences, education, vocation, hobbies, and interests to you? Do you like outdoor activities or museums? Are you content to spend a quiet evening playing Scrabble, or do you like to go dancing and out on the town?

Take a minute and pretend that you are placing a personal ad in your local newspaper. (I am not recommending you really do this, although some women have found interesting companions this way.) Creating a concise description is one way to clarify your dating desires. You might write something like, "Intelligent, witty, attractive single mom in her thirties looking for a sensitive, fun-loving man to share long walks, lively talks, and a good movie now and then." Get creative. If you do ever place an ad, do not give out your address, phone number, or name. Use a post office box number or answering service for any initial correspondence, and use good sense and caution if you decide to follow up on any responses.

SEVEN

Send in the Crones

> How beautiful are the children
> breaking off floating off!
> Like jellyfish budding,
> like seeds from a milkweed pod
>
> blowing   and sailing
> away

—From "Leaving" by Margery Cavanagh

LESSONS IN LETTING GO

I've discovered that motherhood is one continuous lesson in letting go. Our children's first steps, first words, first day at school, first time at camp, first love, are all experiences that lead them into their own lives, into who they are becoming, separate from us. As the poet Kahlil Gibran reminds us, our children are not ours to keep, they come "through us," with souls that "dwell in the house of tomorrow." They are the future. This is as it should be, yet my heart still tears a little each time I say another good-bye to Jessica. As I finish this book, she is getting ready to leave for graduate school in California, and we will say good-bye again.

I was no longer a single mother when Jessica first moved out of the house ten years ago to go to school, but I was consumed with the same solitary need to protect her that filled me when she was a baby and it was just the two of us. I remember sitting alone in the low light of the living-room lamp for most of the night after her high school graduation, holding myself and rocking back and forth, back and forth, like I used to rock her. It felt like the beginning of an end. Soon she'd leave for college, and my emotions were all over the map. I felt foolish and selfish and sad. Yet I also felt happy and excited for her as she got ready to head out on this life adventure. She was a confident and capable young woman, ready to test her wings. Why was I having so much trouble letting her fly?

> Letting go is the realization that you cannot protect your child from the hurts of the world anymore, that you cannot kiss away bruised emotions from failed friendships, from first loves ending, from loneliness.

Whatever metaphor you chose in chapter 1 to describe "family," your description probably contained some sense of connection. Family members hang in delicate balance with each other, like the arms of a mobile. When a change occurs (such as a child leaving home), the balance shifts, and all members are affected. We're not sure what to expect and hang in uneven suspension for a while until we get used to the new reality. Harriet Lerner references Elizabeth Carter's book *Changing Family Life Cycle,* in which Carter mentions how divorce rates soar after children are born and when they leave home. These are "the two transitions that require the greatest emotional and behavioral shifts," writes Lerner.

> I became a single mother when my daughter was in college. My husband and I had fallen out of love long before that, but we were still friends and decided to stay together until she was ready to be on her own. It was a small (but civilized) "implosion" of our family. We went our separate ways but still stay very connected and supportive of each other.

Our society doesn't do a very good job of marking life passages. Traditionally, rites of passage symbolized the death of one life stage and the birth of the next phase. In some tribal societies, members go through a separation ritual, then undergo some physical or psychological test (such as killing an animal or going on a vision quest), and finally rejoin their tribe where they are welcomed as new, transformed individuals. We have graduation ceremonies and parties, but we usually have no public ceremony in which we pass the torch (and the stories and responsibilities) of one generation to the next. For the majority of young people in this country, adulthood is an ambiguous state. There is no magic moment (either chronological or physiological) when a child grows up and no clear understanding of when parents should let go of their children. In traditional rites of passage, a parent publicly and symbolically releases a child. With the exception of a wedding ceremony where the parents might "give away" their children, there are no customs in our society to help parents and children when children leave home. This lack of direction can make it especially hard for single mothers who may struggle with loneliness or identity confusion as their roles change from caretaker to cheerleader when their children move out.

We don't want our daughters to go through some scarification ritual or our sons to have to kill a lion so it will be easier to let them pass into their next life stage, but special ceremonies that symbolize the transitions we are all going through can help us accept those changes. Ceremony and ritual provide an illusion of certainty. We act as if we know and understand what is coming. As this single mom and her daughter found, even a casual ceremony gives us an opportunity to talk about our feelings and acknowledge that we know our lives are changing in some way:

> When my daughter graduated from college, she and I gathered our women friends for a special ceremony. Each participant was asked to bring something—a bit of

wisdom, a poem, a story, or a special object—to share with my daughter. The younger women had been reluctant to participate at all, so we weren't sure how this would work. I spoke first, and then, one by one, each woman took a turn. The older women told stories of challenges they had faced and dreams they had chased. The younger women shared their hopes and wishes for my daughter. It became this remarkable council of women.

Ritual and ceremony gave me a way to calm the conflicting emotions that bubbled in me before Jessica left for college. I couldn't imagine our house without Jessica and her friends popping in and out, and I was a little nervous about what this meant for Michael and me, since this would be the first time in our marriage that we would be alone. It had been the three of us since he joined my little family.

We decided to invite my parents and about twenty of our friends to a St. Paul park to publicly recognize our family's transition. First, I gave Jessica a scissors and an apron that my grandmother had embroidered. She ceremoniously cut the apron string to the applause of a community that loved her. Then Michael and I read vows we had written that acknowledged how our lives were changing. My mother read a blessing, Jessica recited a poem, and those who chose to spoke their thoughts and feelings. I felt like I was getting a transfusion of love and support. It was still hard to say good-bye to Jessica the day she left, but I felt certain we'd all be okay.

Of course, reactions to the thought of an empty nest are as varied as the respondents. Some of my single mother friends were thrilled when their children moved out of the house, because it finally meant that they would have unencumbered time for themselves to explore new interests or just relax in a now quiet home. Some filled their newly found free time by volunteering in their communities. One of my single mother friends decided to rent out one of her bedrooms so she would have company and help with her house payment. Others found the adjustment to empty nesting more difficult.

My son lived with me before he got married, and it has been a tough transition for me. The wedding itself was hard because I was alone, and it was difficult being around my ex-husband and his wife at all the activities. And now my house feels very empty with my son gone. I'm trying to keep busy and do things with friends. I finally went back to see my therapist, and that's helping a lot.

You might feel excited one day and distraught the next day about the prospect of launching your children. Many mothers (including me) find that the doors on their homes are revolving ones when it comes to their children moving in and out. While the first good-bye is the hardest, each subsequent departure gets easier.

I've been a single mom for the majority of my daughter's twenty-five years, so we'd been inseparable up until she left for college. I was devastated at first but soon got used to living alone. She came back home for a while after college, and I have to admit that it was fine when she left this time to move in with her friends. I liked getting my privacy back. We're great friends and see each other at least once a week to have lunch or go shopping. Last December, we took a cruise and reinstated one of our Christmas traditions from my daughter's childhood. We made a paper chain and tore a link off each day to count down the days until we left.

Some of my friends who are single mothers accepted their empty nests as a challenge and opportunity to test their own independence. One friend went to Ireland, where she rode a horse through the Irish countryside alone, plotting her course from inn to inn. Another, who became a single mother when her husband died, got her driver's license at age sixty-five.

There's no right or wrong way to feel about your children leaving home. The important thing is to take care of yourself, gather your circle of support around you when you need to, and seek professional help if you can't shake your feelings of despair.

TAKE A MINUTE

Designing a Rite of Passage

Ritual and ceremony can offer some comfort and reassurance as we let go of one stage of life and move into the next. A rite of passage celebrates who you are at a particular time in your life and honors who you are becoming. A ceremony gives you a way to ask your family and friends for their support and guidance as you embark on a new adventure.

Take a minute and think about a life passage of your own that you would like to acknowledge. (You may want to design a ceremony for your children at some point, but for now, focus on yourself and your passage.) Are you beginning a new life after a divorce? Is your last child moving out of your home? Are you starting a new job or going back to school?

Whom would you like to invite to celebrate your rite of passage? What would you like to happen? Do you want to express your hopes and fears and get emotional support from your community? Do you want to celebrate an event or transition? What preparation do you need to do for your ceremony? Would you like someone to read an opening poem? Do you want to include music? Do you want the participants to bring or prepare anything for the ceremony, such as a poem or an object that symbolizes their wishes for you, or do you want their participation to be spontaneous and more casual? How do you want to close the ceremony? Will you have food and beverages afterward?

In her book *Circle of Stones*, author Judith Duerk asks: "How might it have been different for you if, on your first menstrual day, your mother had given you a bouquet of flowers and taken you to lunch, and then the two of you had gone to meet your father at the jeweler, where your ears were pierced, and your father bought you your first pair of earrings, and then you went with a few of your friends and your mother's friends to get your first lip coloring; and then you went, for the very first time, to the Women's Lodge, to learn the wisdom of the women?"

How does the idea of a ceremony of your own feel to you? Do you think ceremonies could make a difference in your life?

CHANGING BODIES, CHANGING LIVES

As our children go through their various ages and stages, we go through changes of our own, and some of these changes are physical. For many women, the onset of an empty nest co-incides with the onset of perimenopause—a time of irregular periods, hot flashes, and other changes that precede menopause (the date of our final menstrual period). Most women begin perimenopause in their mid-forties and reach menopause in their early fifties, but this is just an average. Some women experience early menopause, and some are much older when the "change," as it is often called, occurs.

While most women have few overall problems with the menopausal process, you might experience some frustrations and inconveniences as your hormone levels fluctuate. I entered perimenopause as Jessica entered adulthood. I bled heavily and had frequent insomnia, two conditions that exaggerated whatever I was feeling about my daughter's woman-hood. Even though I didn't want to have another child at that time in my life, the knowledge that I was approaching a time when I could no longer conceive, coupled with the realization that my daughter was no longer a child, saddened me. I had this primal need to hold a baby, and when I missed a period, I was filled with an irrational hope that I just might be pregnant.

While menopause is something all women go through, I mention it in this book for single mothers because I think it is important that you pay attention to your body as well as your emotions when you experience significant changes such as your children leaving home. The better prepared you are, the smoother these transitions will be. Women who are isolated, without friends or a support group to share their feelings, are much more susceptible to the fears and misinformation that surround menopause. Find a good gynecologist and a supportive circle of friends to help make this time of your life something to celebrate rather than something to endure.

SINGLE GRANDMOTHERS

I went to a wedding recently where the bride and groom, in
addition to being single parents themselves, were both children of single mothers. Like many adult children of single parents I've met, they were cautious about marriage. Although
they had a child together, they chose to wait to get married
until they were certain they were ready to make such a life commitment. Some of the bride's and groom's parents had been
married more than once, and I got confused early on about
which stepparent went with which half-sibling. What struck
me most about this blended and joyful family was the unself-
conscious love everyone showered on the bride and groom's
little boy. I heard more than one guest echo a remark I made
myself, "You can never have too many grandparents." The
grandmothers (both of whom were still single) had an obviously close bond with the child, who went from one to the
other with outstretched arms and adoring eyes.

I'm convinced that good single mothers can make great
grandmothers. The strength and sensitivity they garnered
from their own experiences in mothering can turn them into
pillars of support and wisdom when it comes to nurturing
their children's children.

> I love having my grandson stay with me, and it gives
> my son and his wife time off now and then. I still re-
> member how grateful I was when someone offered to
> watch the kids so I could have some time for myself,
> and, selfishly, it gives me a special chance to have some
> one-to-one time with my grandson. We go to movies, go
> miniature golfing, and sometimes we just hang out and
> talk. He's a great little friend.

When you become a grandmother, you become a seam-
stress of history. You weave the best threads of yesterday into
the bright hope of tomorrow.

We just celebrated my granddaughter's first birthday, so our family rituals continue. The entire family will be going on a special vacation together this June. Although the kids have had many other parental units in their lives, given that their father has been married four times, those relationships have been more like special aunts and uncles. In spite of the many changes, our core family has continued to foster a family connection and maintain our traditional rituals.

Mary Pipher says in her book *Another Country: Navigating the Emotional Terrain of Our Elders*, "The main job for grandparents is to love the kids. But they often help parents keep things in perspective. A grandmother can remind the distraught mother of a teenager, 'You were difficult, too. . . .' As a psychology teacher of undergraduates, I read many papers about grandparents. To many of my students, grandparents equaled love and security. Particularly if the students came from troubled homes—and who doesn't in the 1990s?—the grandparents often represent ritual, continuity, and serenity. The grandparent/grandchild relationship may be the purest relationship that we humans have."

Even single mothers who had a rocky relationship with their own children often have a terrific time with their grandchildren, as this daughter of a single mother reports:

My mother and I have a careful and affectionate dialogue. We are not really close intimates, but she helps me whenever I ask. She is much closer to my children. She lavishes them with gifts and attention when they are together. They love her, and she adores them. She and I spend more time talking about my girls than we do about me, because it's easier for both of us, but I know she loves me. In many ways, my daughters and I are the best things in her life.

Novelist Lillian Smith wrote in *Mother to Daughter, Daughter to Mother,* "Grandma was a kind of first-aid station, or a Red Cross nurse, who took up where the battle ended, accepting us and our little sobbing sins, gathering the whole of us into her lap, restoring us to health and confidence by her amazing faith in life and in a mortal's strength to meet it." Smith could be describing so many of the single mothers I have come to know—mothers who will be grandmothers someday, passing on their wisdom of what it means to be a family.

PARENTING OUR PARENTS

Single mothers are daughters too, and many find that although their maternal responsibilities lessen as their children grow up, their daughterly duties increase. In this country, the job of caring for the elderly most often falls to women. No matter how willing you are to accept that job, taking care of aging, chronically ill, or disabled parents can be emotionally and physically draining. For working single mothers who still have children at home, the task of caring for an aged parent can be overwhelming. For single mothers of grown children who may be thinking, "It's finally my turn for myself," the thought of putting their personal plans on hold so they can take care of a parent can be depressing.

> I love my mom, but I get a little resentful about caring for her sometimes. She gets very confused, so I have to go over to her apartment every morning to make sure she takes her medicine and do other things for her. My children are grown and out of the house, and I had fantasies about taking classes, going on interesting trips, and just having time for myself, but I'm afraid to leave her.

If you are a primary caregiver for an elderly parent, know that your feelings, however complex and confusing they may be, are shared by millions of other caregivers. Whether or not a parent lives with us, being involved in his or her care requires adjustments on everyone's part. Frequently, both the caregiver and the parent lose freedom and privacy. Sometimes it is necessary to handle our parents' financial affairs, and sometimes we take on aspects of their physical care. In some cases, it makes sense for a widowed parent to move in with a daughter and her children when the other parent dies. If the surviving parent is healthy, he or she often helps with child care and other responsibilities, which helps the single mother and gives the children a chance to know their grandparent better.

> My father was always there for my daughter and me, especially after my mom died. He was the best grandpa in the world and always made her feel special. Since she was the only grandchild for many years, they had a special relationship. They would go shopping, make crafts, eat ice cream, and play flashlight tag. My daughter is an adult now, and my dad just died, but I'm so grateful that she has wonderful, special memories from their times together.

In other cases, a parent and daughter might realize that living together isn't a good idea.

> My mom lived out of state when she got cancer, and we both thought it would be a good idea for her to move in with me. We tried it for a while, but it just didn't work. We were both so on edge and soon realized that we had to make other arrangements if we wanted to maintain any kind of close relationship. We found a great nursing home that was more like a house than a hospital, with a garden in the backyard and a nice sitting room for visitors. She felt more independent, and I saw her all the time. I was so glad we were able to be honest with each other and stay close. She died in my arms.

While the need for assistance can be sudden and unforeseen (as the result of a stroke or a heart attack, for example), elderly parents and their children often have time to plan ahead so everyone involved is comfortable with whatever care arrangement is chosen. Even though you can't anticipate everything, each family member should have an opportunity to voice his or her feelings before a crisis develops. Ideally, you can have such a family meeting when your parents are still in good physical and mental health. If you have brothers and sisters who live out of state, try to discuss such things in person when they are in town for a visit. If your children still live at home, it is important to find out how they feel about grandma or grandpa moving in if that is a consideration. If it is difficult for your family to communicate well, you may want to ask a trusted third party (such as a social worker, family counselor, or financial planner) to join you. If possible, this person should be someone who has had experience dealing with the problems under discussion.

My family got what we call the kick in the butt we needed, when my seventy-eight-year-old mom recently had a small stroke. My dad has congestive heart disease, but my mom has always been strong, alert, and tireless. She parasailed in Mexico when she turned sixty, and she researched dad's condition on the Internet when she got a computer a few years ago. In fact, she had her stroke in the middle of a bowling tournament. She lost the ability to speak but kept on bowling until her symptoms became obvious to her teammates, and they called an ambulance. "I didn't want to worry anyone, and I was doing so well," she told us a couple days later. "I had five spares, but I can only remember three of them."

Mom has recovered nicely, but the stroke scared us all. She immediately clicked into gear and had an attorney draw up the necessary documents to protect her and my dad in case of an emergency. She is refreshingly practical about making sound decisions for their future housing and medical care and insists that all matters be discussed openly and honestly with my dad, my two siblings, and me. I've dreaded the time when we would have to deal with such things, but I am discovering that this planning is bringing us closer as a family.

Try to keep the lines of communication open with your family members when it comes time to plan for the care of an elderly parent. Recognize that emotions and stress can run high, and get your personal support system in place so you can get the care *you* need when you need it. Expect to feel a wide range of emotions (guilt, grief, anger, nostalgia, jealousy, fear, etc.) when you meet with your parents and siblings. Sometimes it helps to talk about your feelings, both positive and negative, with a trusted, good-listening friend before you meet with your family.

If you do choose to take on some part of the caregiving responsibilities for an aging parent, be clear about what such duties will entail and ask for the help you will need. Enlist your siblings to help you, and be as specific as possible with each other about what each of you will do. If friends or relatives offer to help, be ready with a list of things they might do. ("Could you visit Mom on Sunday so I can go to my son's ball game?" "Could you help Dad write out his Christmas cards?")

Most communities have a variety of services available for elderly people and their caregivers, such as Meals on Wheels, adult day-care centers, and transportation services. Some churches also provide help to parishioners who need it. There are a number of support groups available where caregivers can meet with other caregivers to share advice, comfort, and companionship. Area Agencies on Aging are good places to start to investigate what services are available to you and your family. If you cannot find a local office, call the Eldercare Locator at 800-677-1116, Monday through Friday, 9:00 A.M. to 11:00 P.M. eastern standard time to find the agency nearest to you.

My mother has taught me so much about what it means to be a parent. She was a constant source of support for me when I was a single mother, and she and Jessica have a grandmother-granddaughter bond today that was cemented during our time alone. Mom continues to be a best friend and a good mom, so it's hard for me to imagine anyone taking care of her. Sometimes I feel as uncertain and frightened about the future as I did in those first days of single motherhood.

But I've decided to use my mom's stroke as my metaphor for facing these challenges and doubts. Single mothers who are reading these words might also find it helpful as they continue on their own journeys. When the path is uncertain and the answers aren't immediate, I intend to do as my mother taught me: move through the silence with determination and keep on bowling.

EPILOGUE

Coming Full Circle

■   ■   ■

Catching my rhythm, you rode the waves of my song,
and for nine months, in unison, we played on.
Your movements quick and lively. *Allegro.*

Little by little *(poco a poco)* a rhapsody
swelled within me, getting stronger. *Crescendo.*

Sometimes my belly danced as you directed the symphony.
Erratic movement from within. *Staccato.*

And then you emerged to sing your own song.

A capella.

—"Jessica in Me," by Cynthia Orange

I wrote that poem in 1972 when my daughter was just a few
months old, about the time I became a single mother. She is
now a few years older than I was when I gave birth to her, and
(unless I live to over one hundred years) I am beyond middle
age. Ours has been a journey of intimacy and letting go, embracing and releasing, rather like breathing. At times I still
guide her; at other times, she now teaches me. It is a circle
dance.

I had an epiphany about this mother-child dance two
years ago on sabbatical, camping at Scammon's Lagoon in
Baja, Mexico. The lagoon is a protected sanctuary for marine

mammals and migratory birds, and every year California gray whales travel six thousand miles from the icy waters of the Bering Sea to the warm waters of Baja's central Pacific coast. From January through March, the lagoon is a major playground and birthing tub for these great creatures. As Michael and I watched the sunset on the beach where we had pitched our tent, we saw at least five whale spouts far out on the water.

The next morning after breakfast, ten of us from all parts of North America and Mexico clambered into a small passenger skiff to get a closer look at the whales. In every direction, dark forms rolled around sending huge sprays into the air. Juan, the *panguero* who piloted the boat, invited me to take the seat next to him in the stern. He told me how the baby whales often rest on the mother whales' backs, floating, trusting. "The *bambinos*," he said and halted, searching his mental lexicon of English just acquired three months earlier. "Ride. The *bambinos* ride on the mother's back," he said triumphantly. "They," he paused again and folded his hands together as in prayer, tilting his head to rest upon them. "Sleep?" I asked in response to his charming pantomime. "*Si*. Sleep," he repeated, and we smiled at each other, each pleased at our successful, though awkward, communication. On cue, a great gray whale rose to the surface by our little boat, her old back mottled and rough. Her baby floated close, almost touching her.

Mothers and babies. Each week away, I got a little less anxious about being gone, so far away from Jessica, so out of touch. "Symbiosis" my psychologist friend had pronounced when Jessica left to backpack in Europe two years before, and I sobbed with the realization that I had no way of contacting her for five months. She made it sound hopeless—a case of terminal interdependence.

As I watched the great mother whale and her baby, my thoughts drifted to Jessica; however, I was no longer worried.

Jessica swims freely, confidently. And at this time in our lives, it is often she who buoys me, nudges me on to ride the waves.

Before we left on this trip, she wrote me a letter reminding me that life, love, and happiness are fluid. They require movement and risk. She said I taught her that.

Resources and Reading

□　□　□

The following is a list of books and places that single mothers might find interesting or helpful. National organizations can often link you to local agencies.

AGING

Doress, Paula Brown, Diana Laskin Siegal, and the Midlife and Older Women Book Project. *Ourselves, Growing Older: Women Aging with Knowledge and Power*. New York: Simon and Schuster, 1987. Fans of *Our Bodies, Ourselves* will love this thorough and empowering guide on how to take care of yourself during the second half of your life.

Eldercare Locator
(800) 677-1116
Call them Monday through Friday, 9:00 A.M. to 11:00 P.M., eastern standard time to find the nearest Agency on Aging. Area Agencies on Aging can help you locate services available to caregivers and the elderly.

Pipher, Mary. *Another Country: Navigating the Emotional Terrain of Our Elders*. New York: Penguin Putnam, 1999. An interesting and helpful discussion on how lives and relationships change for everyone when parents and grandparents journey into old age, by the author of the best-selling *Reviving Ophelia*.

FAMILIES AND CHILDREN

Boston Women's Health Book Collective. *Ourselves and Our Children: A Book by and for Parents*. New York: Random House, 1978. This book, written by the authors of the now classic *Our Bodies, Ourselves*, weaves stories, poems, and practical advice in a very useful guide for parents of children of all ages.

Center for the Prevention of Sexual and Domestic Violence Web site (www.cpsdv.org). A good Internet site for information on domestic violence and sexual abuse.

Connect for Kids Web site (www.connectforkids.org). An on-line community that provides articles by experts, resources and links to national organizations, a weekly on-line publication of current news and issues that deal with children and families, and an opportunity for on-line discussion. Sponsored by the Benton Foundation.

Coontz, Stephanie. *The Way We Never Were: American Families and the Nostalgia Trap*. New York: Harper Collins, 1992, and *The Way We Really Are: Coming to Terms with America's Changing Families*. New York: Perseus Books, 1997. Coontz debunks the myth of family by offering a historical and sociological perspective that entertains and informs.

Elkind, David. *All Grown Up and No Place to Go: Teenagers in Crisis*. Reading, Mass.: Addison-Wesley Publishing Company, 1984, and *The Hurried Child: Growing Up Too Fast Too Soon*. Reading, Mass.: Addison-Wesley Publishing Company, 1981. Elkind is a professor of child study at Tufts University who tackles the problems of children and teens as they struggle to cope in a turbulent society.

Federal Office of Child Support Enforcement Web site (202) 401-9200; Internet address: www.acf.dhhs.gov/programs/cse

You can find your local and state offices of child support enforcement by calling this number or checking this Web site; current information about laws regarding child support is also available.

Herman, Marina Lachecki, Ann Schimpf, Joseph Passineau, and Paul Treuer. *Teaching Kids to Love the Earth.* Duluth, Minn.: Pfeifer-Hamilton, 1991. This books includes 186 outdoor activities for children of all ages, with accompanying stories and instructions designed to instill an appreciation and love of nature.

National Association for the Education of Young Children Web site (www.naeyc.org). Visitors to the NAEYC site can find a complete list of places that offer accredited Early Childhood Family Education classes.

National Domestic Violence Hotline
(800) 799-7233
The National Domestic Violence Hotline links individuals to help in their area using a nationwide database that includes detailed information on domestic violence shelters, other emergency shelters, legal advocacy and assistance programs, and social service programs. One call summons immediate help, in English or Spanish, twenty-four hours a day, seven days a week, and interpreters are available to translate an additional 139 languages. The hotline may be reached toll free from all fifty states, the District of Columbia, Puerto Rico, and the U.S. Virgin Islands.

Roots & Wings Parenting Program
Call Hazelden Information and Educational Services at (800) 328-9000 for information on this parenting program, or see *What to Say or Do . . . From Diapers to Diploma: A Parents Quick Reference Guide.* 2d ed. Center City, Minn.: Hazelden, 2000. This book of practical parenting tips grew out of the *Roots & Wings* program.

Today's Gift: Daily Meditations for Families. Center City, Minn.: Hazelden, 1985. A daily meditation book designed to help family members talk about their thoughts and feelings.

U.S. Department of Education's Safe and Drug-Free Schools Program
(877) 4EDPUBS; Internet address: www.ed.gov/offices/OESE/SDFS
Call or log on for your free copy of *Growing Up Drug-Free: A Parent's Guide to Prevention.*

U.S. Department of Labor
(800) 959-FMLA
Contact this department to get information on the federal Family and Medical Leave Act.

MENTORING PROGRAMS

Big Brothers Big Sisters of America
230 North Thirteenth Street
Philadelphia, PA 19107
(215) 567-7000; Internet address: www.bbbsa.org
Founded in 1904, this is the nation's oldest and largest youth mentoring organization with programs in all fifty states.

National Mentoring Partnership
1600 Duke Street, Suite 300
Alexandria, VA 22314
(703) 224-2200; Internet address: www.mentoring.org
A national organization that offers training and information to communities, schools, businesses, civic associations, churches, and other organizations that want to establish mentor programs.

Save the Children mentor programs
1-877-Be-A-MENTOR

Save the Children is a well-respected organization that works to better the lives of children throughout the world. They also maintain a national mentoring hotline that provides information to callers who are searching for mentors or who want to volunteer as mentors.

Your Time—Their Future
(800) 788-2800; Internet address: www.health.org/yourtime
A Substance Abuse and Mental Health Services Administration (SAMHSA) campaign that features mentoring and volunteer opportunities for adults.

PARENTING

Alexander, Shoshana. *In Praise of Single Parents: Mothers and Fathers Embracing the Challenge.* New York: Houghton Mifflin Company, 1994. Alexander draws on her own experiences and the experiences of other single mothers to discuss the joys and challenges of single parenting.

Engber, Andrea, and Leah Klungness. *The Complete Single Mother: Reassuring Answers to Your Most Challenging Concerns.* Holbrook, Mass.: Adams Publishing, 1995. A practical "encyclopedia" for single mothers that covers a wide range of issues such as donor insemination, divorce, child development, finances, and dating.

Lamott, Anne. *Operating Instructions: A Journal of My Son's First Year.* New York: Ballantine Books, 1993. This is a poignant, often hilarious, account of a single mother's first year as a parent. Women of all ages and stages of parenting should enjoy this book.

Lerner, Harriet. *The Mother Dance: How Children Change Your Life.* New York: HarperCollins, 1999. Lerner (the author of *The Dance of Anger*) pulls no punches about what it means to be a mother, but she does so in an engaging way that makes you feel like you are part of the conversation.

Making Lemonade Web site (www.makinglemonade.com). A single-parent network founded by Jody Seidler, a single mother who facilitates educational groups for single parents and their children.

Moms On Line Web site (www.momsonline.com). A resource and network for mothers in conjunction with America Online.

National Organization of Single Mothers (NOSM)
P.O. Box 68
Midland, NC 28107-0068
(704) 888-KIDS; Internet address: www.singlemothers.org
A clearinghouse of information and network of support for single mothers; founded in 1991 by single mother Andrea Engber (coauthor of *The Complete Single Mother*).

Parents Place Web site (www.parentsplace.com/family/singleparent). A good site for interesting articles and other information on single parenting.

Parents without Partners, Inc.
1650 South Dixie Highway, Suite 510
Boca Raton, FL 33432
(800) 637-7974; Internet address: www.parentswithoutpartners.org
A national organization founded in 1957 (with many local affiliates) for divorced and widowed parents.

Single Mothers by Choice (SMC)
P.O. Box 1642
Gracie Square Station
New York, NY 10028
(212) 988-0993; E-mail: mattes@pipeline.com
Founded in 1981 by Jane Mattes, a psychotherapist and single mother, SMC provides information and support to single mothers as well as to women contemplating or trying to achieve single motherhood.

Single Rose Web site (www.singlerose.com). A resource for divorced, widowed, and never-been-married women who are raising children alone that offers articles on a variety of topics and an opportunity for visitors to connect with each other.

S E L F - C A R E

Al-Anon
(888) 4AL-ANON; Internet address: www.al-anon.org
Call Al-Anon to find out the locations and times of meetings in your area or to get information about Alateen or Alatot support groups.

Burns, David D., *Feeling Good: The New Mood Therapy*. Rev. ed. New York: Avon Books, 1999. Burns offers ways to develop a positive outlook that helps you feel better about yourself and your life.

Cameron, Julia. *The Artist's Way: A Spiritual Path to Higher Creativity*. New York: Jeremy P. Tarcher/Perigee, 1992. A twelve-week self-study course to ignite your creativity and enhance your spiritual growth.

Campaign on Clinical Depression
(800) 228-1114
Provides free information on depression, its treatment, and local screening sites.

Center for Substance Abuse Treatment hotline
(800) 662-HELP
A twenty-four-hour service of the Substance Abuse and Mental Health Services Administration (SAMHSA) that links callers to a variety of hotlines that provide treatment referrals.

Clarke, Jean Illsley. *Self-Esteem: A Family Affair*. 1978. Reprint, Center City, Minn.: Hazelden, 1998. Clarke maintains that self-esteem starts at home in the nurturing interaction between children and adults, and she offers creative ways to help all family members build their individual self-esteem.

Federal Student Aid Information Center
(800) 433-3243
A good place to start to see what financial aid might be available to you if you are thinking about going back to school.

National Mental Health Association Web site (www.depression-screening.org). A confidential screening for depression that helps people determine if they should seek medical help.

United Way
701 North Fairfax Street
Alexandria, VA 22314-2045
(703) 836-7100; Internet address: www.unitedway.org
You can also check your phone directory to find your local United Way agency. Their "First Call for Help" directory is a valuable resource for finding support services in your area.

SPIRITUALITY, RITUAL, AND CEREMONY

Baldwin, Christina. *Life's Companion: Journal Writing as a Spiritual Quest*. New York: Bantam Books, 1990. Baldwin gives seekers the tools and inspiration they need to find and cultivate their spiritual center.

Baylor, Byrd. *I'm in Charge of Celebrations*. New York: Charles Scribner's Sons, 1986. A beautiful children's book that encourages people to mark their own special days (such as Rainbow Celebration Day) and ultimately celebrate themselves.

Casey, Karen. *Each Day a New Beginning*. Center City, Minn.: Hazelden, 1982. One of the most popular daily meditation books for women.

Cox, Meg. *The Heart of a Family: Searching America for New Traditions That Fulfill Us*. New York: Random House, 1998. Cox interviewed more than two hundred families around the country to find what works and what doesn't in ritual and how modern families can create their own rituals to reflect and celebrate their lives.

Hammerschlag, Carl A., and Howard D. Silverman. *Healing Ceremonies: Creating Personal Rituals for Spiritual, Emotional, Physical, and Mental Health*. New York: Berkley Publishing Company, 1997. Two physicians explore how personal ceremonies can build mental, emotional, physical, and spiritual health.

Schaef, Anne Wilson. *Meditations for Women Who Do Too Much*. San Francisco: Harper and Row, 1990. This book is a daily reminder to busy women to slow down and take care of themselves.

Solly, Richard, and Roseann Lloyd. *Journey Notes: Writing for Recovery and Spiritual Growth*. Center City, Minn.: Hazelden, 1989. These creative writing teachers offer useful and inspirational guidance on how to use a journal in your quest for inner growth and healing.

Bibliography

Alexander, Shoshana. *In Praise of Single Parents: Mothers and Fathers Embracing the Challenge.* New York: Houghton Mifflin Company, 1994.

Baldwin, Christina. *Calling the Circle: The First and Future Culture.* Newberg, Ore.: Swan-Raven, 1994.

———. *Life's Companion: Journal Writing as a Spiritual Quest.* New York: Bantam Books, 1990.

Baldwin, Christina, and Cynthia Orange. *New Life, New Friends: Making and Keeping Relationships in Recovery.* New York: Bantam Books, 1993.

Boston Women's Health Book Collective. *Ourselves and Our Children: A Book by and for Parents.* New York: Random House, 1978.

Burns, David D. *Feeling Good: The New Mood Therapy.* Rev. ed. New York: Avon Books, 1999.

Cameron, Julia. *The Artist's Way: A Spiritual Path to Higher Creativity.* New York: Jeremy P. Tarcher/Perigee, 1992.

Children's Defense Fund. "Poor Children Come in All Colors and Live in Every Family Type and Geographic Area of America." In *The State of America's Children Yearbook 2000.* Available on-line: http://www.childrensdefense.org/greenbook00_stats.html [Accessed September 2000].

Clarke, Jean Illsley. *Self-Esteem: A Family Affair.* 1978. Reprint, Center City, Minn.: Hazelden, 1998.

Coontz, Stephanie. *The Way We Never Were: American Families and the Nostalgia Trap.* New York: Harper Collins, 1992.

———. *The Way We Really Are: Coming to Terms with America's Changing Families.* New York: Perseus Books, 1997.

Dickson, Charles. "Learning Human Relations from Geese." *The American Legion Magazine,* December 1999.

Doress, Paula Brown, Diana Laskin Siegal, and the Midlife and Older Women Book Project. *Ourselves, Growing Older: Women Aging with Knowledge and Power.* New York: Simon and Schuster, 1987.

Duerk, Judith. *Circle of Stones: Woman's Journey to Herself.* San Diego: LuraMedia, 1989.

Elkind, David. *All Grown Up and No Place to Go: Teenagers in Crisis.* Reading, Mass.: Addison-Wesley Publishing Company, 1984.

———. *The Hurried Child: Growing Up Too Fast Too Soon.* Reading, Mass.: Addison-Wesley Publishing Company, 1981.

Engber, Andrea, and Leah Klungness. *The Complete Single Mother: Reassuring Answers to Your Most Challenging Concerns.* Holbrook, Mass.: Adams Publishing, 1995.

Erbe, Bonnie. "Traditional Families Are Extinct." *Saint Paul Pioneer Press* (21 October 1990). Quoted in Viqi Wagner and Karin Swisher, eds. *The Family in America: Opposing Viewpoints.* San Diego: Greenhaven Press, 1992.

Garbarino, James. *Lost Boys: Why Our Sons Turn Violent and How We Can Save Them.* New York: Simon and Schuster, 1999.

Herzog, James, Charles Flatter, Phyllis Tyson, and Katherine Ross. "Mother's Love: How Women Nurture Their Children through the Years." Sesame Street Parents, Children's Television Workshop.

Available on-line: http://www.sesamestreet.org/parents/advice/article/0,4125,47960,00.html [Accessed 11 April 2000].

Karr, Mary. "Dysfunctional Nation." *New York Times Magazine,* 12 May 1996, sec. 6, p. 70.

Lamott, Anne. *Operating Instructions: A Journal of My Son's First Year.* New York: Ballantine Books, 1993.

Lansky, Vicki. "Divorce: Ten Things Your Mother Never Told You." Divorce Online. Available on-line: http://www.divorceonline.com/articles/32268.html [Accessed September 2000].

Lerner, Harriet. *The Mother Dance: How Children Change Your Life.* New York: HarperCollins, 1999.

Louv, Richard. "New Single Parent Networks." Connect for Kids, Benton Foundation. Available on-line: http://www.connectforkids.org [Accessed September 2000].

Major, A. Jayne. "Stress Busting for Single Parents: Moving from Struggle to Cooperation." Making Lemonade. Available on-line: http://www.makinglemonade.com/newcreative/stressbust.htm [Accessed September 2000].

Mattes, Jane. *Single Mothers by Choice: A Guidebook for Single Women Who Are Considering or Have Chosen Motherhood.* New York: Random House, 1994.

National Center for Health Statistics. "Births in the U.S. Increase for the First Time Since 1990." Press release, 28 March 2000.

Olsen, Tillie. *Mother to Daughter, Daughter to Mother: Mothers on Mothering—A Daybook and a Reader.* New York: Feminist Press, 1984.

Orange, Cynthia. "The Importance of Rites of Passage for Adolescents and Young Adults." Master's thesis, Hamline University, 1993.

Palmer, Parker J. *Let Your Life Speak: Listening for the Voice of Vocation.* San Francisco: Jossey-Bass, 2000.

"Parenting Is Prevention." Advertising supplement. Office of National Drug Control Policy and U.S. Department of Health and Human Services, n.d.

Parents without Partners, International. "Facts about Single-Parent Families." Available on-line: http://www.parentswithout partners.org [Accessed 13 March 2000].

Pipher, Mary. *Another Country: Navigating the Emotional Terrain of Our Elders.* New York: Penguin Putnam, 1999.

———. *The Shelter of Each Other: Rebuilding Our Families.* New York: G. P. Putnam, 1996.

Pogrebin, Letty Cottin. *Family Politics: Love and Power on an Intimate Frontier.* New York: McGraw-Hill Book Company, 1983.

Roots & Wings: Raising Resilient Children Parent Handbook. Rev. ed. Center City, Minn.: Hazelden, 2000.

Rosenfeld, Isadore. "When the Sadness Won't Go Away." *Parade Magazine,* 19 September 1999.

Save the Children. "U.S. Children Are at Risk." Available on-line: http://www.savethechildren.org/usw1.html [Accessed September 2000].

Schaef, Anne Wilson. *Meditations for Women Who Do Too Much.* San Francisco: Harper and Row, 1990.

Smith, Lynn. "Dad's Absence Isn't Always Bad." *Seattle Times,* 15 August 1997.

Stacey, Judith. *Brave New Families: Stories of Domestic Upheaval in Late-Twentieth-Century America.* Berkeley: Basic Books, 1990; University of California Press, 1998.

Steele, Claude M. "Thin Ice: 'Stereotype Threat' and Black College Students." *The Atlantic Monthly,* August 1999, 44–54.

Today's Gift: Daily Meditations for Families. Center City, Minn.: Hazelden, 1985.

U.S. Bureau of the Census. "Marital Status and Living Arrangements: March 1998 (Update)." *Current Population Reports,* P20–514. Washington, D.C.: U.S. Government Printing Office, 1998.

What to Say or Do . . . From Diapers to Diploma: A Parents Quick Reference Guide. 2d ed. Center City, Minn.: Hazelden, 2000.

Index

About the Author

Cynthia Orange is a writer, editor, and writing consultant. She teaches creative writing at the Loft Literary Center in Minneapolis and the University of Minnesota Compleat Scholar. She has received awards for poetry, creative nonfiction, essays, and newspaper articles. She coauthored *New Life, New Friends* with Christina Baldwin (Bantam 1993) and is one of the authors of the meditation book *Today's Gift* (Hazelden 1985). She has also published over 450 articles, columns, and guest editorials in a number of newspapers, magazines, and literary journals. She lives in West St. Paul, Minnesota.

HAZELDEN INFORMATION AND EDUCATIONAL SERVICES
is a division of the Hazelden Foundation, a not-for-profit organization. Since 1949, Hazelden has been a leader in promoting the dignity and treatment of people afflicted with the disease of chemical dependency.

The mission of the foundation is to improve the quality of life for individuals, families, and communities by providing a national continuum of information, education, and recovery services that are widely accessible; to advance the field through research and training; and to improve our quality and effectiveness through continuous improvement and innovation.

Stemming from that, the mission of this division is to provide quality information and support to people wherever they may be in their personal journey—from education and early intervention, through treatment and recovery, to personal and spiritual growth.

Although our treatment programs do not necessarily use everything Hazelden publishes, our bibliotherapeutic materials support our mission and the Twelve Step philosophy upon which it is based. We encourage your comments and feedback.

The headquarters of the Hazelden Foundation are in Center City, Minnesota. Additional treatment facilities are located in Chicago, Illinois; New York, New York; Plymouth, Minnesota; St. Paul, Minnesota; and West Palm Beach, Florida. At these sites, we provide a continuum of care for men and women of all ages. Our Plymouth facility is designed specifically for youth and families.

For more information on Hazelden, please call **1-800-257-7800.** Or you may access our World Wide Web site on the Internet at **http://www.hazelden.org.**